Lighten Up

Managing With Mirth Ain't Rocket Surgery

Scott Christopher

Bloomington, IN

authorHOUSE

Milton Keynes, UK

AuthorHouse™
1663 Liberty Drive, Suite 200
Bloomington, IN 47403
www.authorhouse.com
Phone: 1-800-839-8640

AuthorHouse™ UK Ltd.
500 Avebury Boulevard
Central Milton Keynes, MK9 2BE
www.authorhouse.co.uk
Phone: 08001974150

First published by AuthorHouse 9/12/2006

ISBN: 1-4259-3621-0 (sc)

Library of Congress Control Number: 2006904658

Printed in the United States of America
Bloomington, Indiana

This book is printed on acid-free paper.

Table of Contents

CHAPTER 1:
The Setup 1

CHAPTER 2
GreatLeaders Get It 13

CHAPTER 3
A Sense of Humor Is Just That..............................25

CHAPTER 4
Discovering Your Levity..33

CHAPTER 5
A Time and Place 47

CHAPTER 6
Crows Feet and Rosy Cheeks.................................59

CHAPTER 7
Good For What Ails You 67

CHAPTER 8
Self-Deprecating Humor 77

CHAPTER 9
Practical Applications of Levity............................87

CHAPTER 10
The Wrap Up 101

ABOUT THE AUTHOR.......................................105

CHAPTER 1:

The Setup

Humor is a funny thing.

Sometime in 1998, my boss at the time, Delroy Wheeze (name changed), came to me and asked me to help him "be funnier." I returned his request with a blank stare. Funni-*er*?

"You want me to teach you how to be funny," I politely re-stated.

"Right. I think I got the other stuff down ok. Now I just need to sharpen that comic edge a little."

"Uh HUH."

Delroy was from a small, farm town in very rural Utah and was intimately unfamiliar with anything comical (except of course his name, which I made up). Additionally, though Delroy had a keen business mind, was a great idea man and mostly had "the other stuff down," we, his employees, mostly viewed him as a hopeless BrowKnitter (we'll discuss this later) and little else. We pretty much only did what Delroy asked because he was the boss. He signed the checks.

"Scott, you're one of the funniest people I know," Delroy said. "If you'd show me how to be funny it could really help me out."

The odd request intrigued me. I didn't actually believe that I could mastermind some Pygmalion-like transformation, though I did secretly entertain thoughts of overtime pay. My job, after all, was head of the public speaking department, not comedy consultant to the management. I promised him I'd work on it and then, like all promises based on in-passing, bizarre, small talk I forgot about it until years after I'd left the company and the leadership dynamo that was Delroy Wheeze.

More recently another boss of mine, Adrian Gostick (real name!), approached me about "funnying up" some of his compelling but otherwise dry presentation material. This time I quickly obliged. Why? I like Adrian. He's a good leader whose demeanor is pleasant and light. In addition, we share a similar taste in humor and it wasn't difficult to imagine the two of us coming up with pretty good material. Plus, I wanted to help. Adrian's one of those people you're happy to follow.

Adrian, and Delroy had both arrived at the same conclusion. They could afford to exercise their humor muscles a little more. One wanted to add it to his overall style, the other, whose style already included levity, simply wanted to enhance a speech. Levity has a special place in the world of leadership. It is the power of perspective- -the need to splash a little color around an otherwise monochromatic environment. Consider the imagery found in the lyrics of this little-known tune:

Some folks view the world as a stone
Concrete daubed in dull monotone

Your heart is a big box of paints

And others, the canvas you're dealt

Awaken you dreamers, adrift in your beds
Balloons and streamers decorate the inside of your heads…

Awaken you dreamers, asleep at your desks
Parrots and lemurs populate your unconscious grotesques…

Please let some out. Do it today.
But don't let the loveless ones sell you a world wrapped in gray.

Andy Partridge

This book is for and about the "dreamers" and the "loveless ones." Those who may have vivid and rich morsels of mirth dancing around their psyches, but don't share them with others.

I'm not talking about repeating verbatim every sophomorically hilarious line from *Dumb and Dumber* in your next production meeting, though that level of levity may work in your office from time to time. It's easier than that.

A question: Why do you have this book? What possessed you to read it? (Ok, *two* questions) Now answer this simple multiple-choice question, for which there is no right or wrong answer. Just answer truthfully.

Why are you reading this book?

A. You want to be funnier at work.

B. You need to lighten up.

C. You want to become a better leader.

D. All of the above

Answer: Although there is no right or wrong answer, the right answer is "C." Actually "B" and "C" are closest to the correct answers. So, let's just do this:

Answer: B and C...even though there is no right or wrong answer.

Here's why "A" is wrong. After reading this book you will not necessarily be funnier. On the other hand, just like those TV commercials from the 70s used to preach, Reading Is Fundamental. You should devour humor books, magazines, and other publications. The more humor you absorb, the greater chance you have of occasionally squeezing some out. But this book, on its own, will not arm you with boffo material.

This is not a joke book for ambitious corporate types. It's not a "how-to" on "knocking 'em dead" at the annual management conference. If you have allusions of becoming a legendary office clown, some kind of Bozo of Building J, put this book down. It's not for you. In keeping with the book's theme, the tone is light and occasionally irreverent, and there are some practical tips for loosening up, but it's not a field guide for budding comedians.

Now, if you suddenly become the next Larry the Cable Guy of the corporate world, I'll be happy to take credit for it, but that is not the purpose of this work. The title "Leading with Levity" says it all. Levity is defined as "lightness of manner." How often have you muttered under your breath, "Lighten up, will ya?" It's usually aimed at a colleague or superior who appears to have a yardstick wedged up a particular orifice.

Humor is a funny thing. Workplace humor...not so much. It's a tightrope act, isn't it?

Leading with Levity is about developing a lightness of manner (and extracting the yardstick). I equate levity with having a *sense* of humor; too many wrongly assume that a sense of humor means

4

you're funny. The sad truth is that very few legitimately funny people can walk the earth at the same time. Funniness is like matter. There is only so much out there. The power to evoke actual laughter and not just charity chuckles is a rare possession indeed. This book is aimed at the majority of us who simply possess or wish to develop a shred of a sense of humor, in the hopes that it will help us develop into stronger leaders.

There is little doubt that a truly effective leader understands and wisely wields the power of levity, and with good reason. The *Harvard Business Review* (September 2003) reported that executives with a sense of humor climb the corporate ladder more quickly and earn more money than their counterparts.

Do you need any more reason than that? And that's just the selfish "me first" mentality. Develop and exercise your sense of humor—lighten up—then hold on for the ride. You'll be behind the wheel of a Hummer and business golfing in Palm Springs faster than you can say "heated, marble toilet seat."

But, why? Will you be promoted solely on the grounds of being witty? You ingratiated yourselves with the big boys because you "slayed" them with a killer bit of wit, but is that really enough to get you a seat on the executive jet? Hardly. Humor, on its own merit, does very little to establish your credibility.

More often than not your success depends on the *people you lead*, and their perception of you as a leader. What exactly can you extract from your workforce? Productivity. On-time delivery. Great ideas. Numbers. Results. Loyalty. Respect. Shall I go on? Ultimately, your humor will move you up the ladder faster because you **lead** your people **with levity**, not because you made JJ Mooney, the CEO, choke with laughter on an olive at the company mixer.

Those savvy managers that can lead a team or department of employees to the promised land of retention, satisfaction, engagement, and productivity have the best shot at promotion and security.

Incidentally, those who lead with levity and laugh regularly seem to enjoy longer and fuller lives.

Leading with levity is not about being funny. It's about being fun. Getting laughs is a bonus. If you can get people to really laugh, it will enhance the levity. So we'll definitely discuss "being funny," but it ranks second in the scheme of things.

There are three groups that need introducing before we proceed:

The JawClenchers aka the TeethGrinders:

A JawClencher (JC) is indigenous to all industries, fields, professions, and disciplines. The JC is a nose-breather, but only by necessity. The mouth remains clamped tight to allow for teeth grinding and/or jaw clenching. The nostrils must flare to facilitate labored, audible nasal breathing. The most obvious evidence of this type of leader is the pulsating rear jawbones, not unlike fish gills, caused by the grinding pressure of the molars.

JawClenchers are known for their hell-bent commitment to sucking any morsel of joy from themselves and everyone around them for the good of the organization. If they were to vocalize their leadership philosophy it would sound something like, "This is WAR, people!" or "If we don't do this right, some of us will be killed!" and, "Wipe that grin off your face, happy boy, this is ain't no laughing matter!"

JCs do not laugh or smile or "blow things off." They are riveted by the deadly seriousness of their mission, and you'd better be too, or else.

What happens to JCs at home on weekends or holidays is anyone's guess. A JC might actually be a fun-loving guy after hours, but certainly not on company time. "Don't you get it? The fate of the world is in our hands!" they seem to say.

If you suspect that you are a JawClencher or have displayed symptoms—read on—it's time to loosen the clench and let a little air flow over your tongue and teeth. JCs are deadly to a company's success. Indications of a high JC atmosphere include low morale, poor production, and attrition. After all, how fun or easy is it to work with people who are wound tighter than Jerry Falwell at a gay pride parade?

Remember this little nugget from the Bill Murray movie, Stripes?

Psycho: *The name's Francis Sawyer, but everybody calls me Psycho. Any of you guys call me Francis, and I'll kill you.*

And I don't like nobody touching my stuff! So just keep your meat hooks off.

If I catch any of you guys in my stuff, I'll kill you. Also, I don't like nobody touching me. Now, any of you homos touch me, and I'll kill you.

Ox *(John Candy): Lighten up, Francis.*

And that pretty much says it all right there: lighten up.

The BrowKnitters aka GlazeEyes:

While JawClenchers are best characterized by the anger/rage/ire of their seriousness at work, BrowKnitters (BKs), are mostly docile in their seriousness. The term derives from the almost constant state of both eyebrows drawn together and downward as if being pinched or knitted together in the middle (think Sting at his pouty best). It is most associated with someone who is lost in deep thought, but can also be indicative of someone who is feeling annoyed. JawClenchers (see above) frequently exhibit BrowKnitting, but it is usually coupled with wild eyes and flared nostrillia (not an actual word, but it sounds smart).

BKs can be either nose or mouth breathers, and on rare occasions, both. These are leaders so engrossed in their work and the "do it or die" mentality, that they quite involuntarily inhale nasally and exhale orally. The ensuing exhalation is often accompanied by an almost whispered but audible "nkuuuhh," as the soft palate is throbbed by the air return. BKs are similar to JCs—but for the threat of violence—in that they simply do not have the time for levity.

I had a BK boss once—the afore-mentioned Delroy Wheeze—that never actually listened to a single word anyone said because he was always so lost in his own work-related thoughts.

Smiles or other expressions of levity only appear when a BK sorts out a problem mentally and thus finds some satisfaction. If co-workers or subordinates display playfulness it is met by indifference from the BK. While employee joking would provoke chastening from a JawClencher, a true BrowKnitter will only return a quizzical knitted, or even raised, brow as if wondering, "What could any of this jocularity have to do with saving the world (the BK's job)?" A BK could also be known as a Glaze-Eye because she gets so consumed by the non-stop torrent of potentially profitable ideas running through her head that she zones into corporate catatonia…even as you speak directly to her.

GreatLeaders Or Leaders Who Get It:

GreatLeaders (GLs) understand the power of leading with levity. These leaders are characterized by an overall sense of lightness, humor, joviality, perspective, love, humanity…you get the idea. They take work seriously. They understand accountability. A GL knows the power of timely and sincere recognition. She knows how to take a joke, how to laugh at herself, and when humor is inappropriate for the time or place.

As early as the mid-1980s, a survey found that 84% of Vice Presidents and personnel directors in 100 of the largest corporations in the country felt that employees with a sense of humor are more effective on the job than people with little or no sense of humor. The organization conducting the survey concluded, "**People with a sense of humor tend to be more creative, less rigid and more willing to consider and embrace new ideas and methods.**"

Think about people you know at work that are creative, flexible, and open to change. How many of them also possess what you consider wit, humor, or levity? Are any of these people in management? If they aren't, is it a stretch to think that they ultimately will be? Wouldn't you be willing to accept these people as your leader?

Another mid-1980s survey of 737 chief executives of major corporations showed that an amazing 98% of those completing the survey said they would hire a person with a good sense of humor over one who seemed to lack a sense of humor. Read that again. Ninety-eight percent of CEOs of major corporations say they would prefer to hire someone with a sense of humor.

Now, you may be choking back the urge to blurt out a resounding "Duh!" It's just so obvious, right? But don't miss the real point of this stat: whom is the CEO hiring? Well, you. I mean, the chief executive really only gets involved in hiring decisions for management and leadership, if then. So, you'd best get a handle on this humor thing before you even get the job. It should be apparent at all levels of the hiring process that you possess some mirth.

Once hired, stay true to what got you there. Most job candidates put on their best game face for the selection process, but sadly, too many do a 180 before they've even unpacked their diplomas and plaques. Unleash some levity to get the job; then, please, for the sake of employee satisfaction and productivity, work to create an environment where others can consistently do the same.

According to the CEO of Rosenbluth International, Hal Rosenbluth, it is "almost inhumane if companies create a climate where people can't naturally have fun . . . Our role and responsibility as leaders and associates is to create a place where people can enjoy themselves. I know our company is doing well when I walk around and hear people laughing."

And on a day-to-day basis, to whom would the credit go if the CEO walks into your department and finds the company "doing well" because he or she hears laughter? Aren't you, as the department leader, the one who sets or squashes the tone? If there is an overall sense of cheer and well-being among a group of coworkers isn't it reasonable to give some, if not all, of the credit to that group's boss?

> *The most productive workplaces have at least ten minutes of laughter every hour."*
> Barbara Glanz, Humor Consultant

At the end of the day this book is about you becoming a better or maybe even a (GreatLeader. Everybody knows one. At some point in your life—in school, at church, at work, even at home—you've had the treat of working for or with a GreatLeader. They inspired you in some way to accomplish something. They were role models to you for your future leadership positions. So all you have to do is figure out what made that person so great and then do the same. Can you dissect those qualities; can you break down the leader?

Come on, top of mind, let's just run a list of what it takes to be a GreatLeader:

> Lead by example,
> know your business,
> laugh a lot,
> be the first to arrive and the last to leave,
> celebrate your people,
> train your workforce,
> define expectations clearly,
> be specific,
> know your people,
> love your people,
> don't talk, listen,

know the market,
know the competition,
anticipate change,
set goals,
plan, plan, plan,
expect improvement,
have a heart,
be fair,
empower your people,
and on and on and on…

The list of leadership traits that qualify a leader to have a bronze bust commissioned (of their head oddly enough, not their bust) and about which thousands of business books have been written is so long that if you were to write each trait on its own square of toilet paper you would have a roll as long as all the lines to all the ladies' rooms at all the NFL stadiums on any Sunday in October.

This book is about just one of those squares of toilet paper.

CHAPTER 2

Great Leaders Get It

"If you would rule the world quietly, you must keep it amused."
Ralph Waldo Emerson

If you've recently been promoted to a position of leadership, congratulations. You now lead a group of people. This is *your* crew. You're the captain. This ship sails under your command and, by golly, sail it will. Ahhhrggh, ya scallywag.

In your excitement to don your tassel-shouldered uniform and Cap'n Crunch hat, in your rush to hoist the mainmast and take the wheel, setting course for the wide open seas of corporate success, in your eager attempt to bark out your first orders to "heave" and "look lively," you realize that you have no idea how to actually get the crew to do all those things.

You don't really connect with your people as a leader, because you've never really needed to. That was someone else's burden. Maybe your promotion to management is more the result of some new-fangled idea you brought to the table than your ability to manage a team of actual humans. Perhaps your recent work significantly contributed to the company's bottom line. You made everybody a little richer, so, wham! here's your reward: a nice, new title along with some added responsibilities.

Let's stay with the pirate ship analogy. You've moved up through the ranks. You started as a mere swabby. Did that for nigh on ten year. Somebody stabbed the Yeoman between the shoulder blades—probably you—and you took that post. Now more'n two score year of sailin' you're moved up to Cap'n, cuz you've outlived the rest...and you've got a killer eye patch and teeth composed of various precious metals.

Maybe that happened at work. You won the battle of attrition. They finally caved; there's nobody left to promote. Everyone else has been run through, metaphorically.

We can't of course ignore that maybe you just flat-out actually deserve this position. You did the education thing, got your MBA, have read all the best-selling business books and attended dozens of CE courses and seminars. You wear "power" attire and can recite the Seven Habits in your sleep, backwards, and in Mandarin. But most importantly, you know the business.

Whatever the case, are you actually qualified to *lead* people? Sure, you know the ropes, years of experience, great track record, bla bla bla. If you had to, you could step in and cover for anybody in the company. You're a Renaissance man or woman. Leading by example is a critical component to be sure, but you technically are no longer a mere peer.

You now are supposed to manage other people, get them to do things, and as great as you've been in your "old" job, it won't mean squat if you can't motivate others to similar levels of success. It's like starting all over again. Like when the NBA playoffs begin. Forget about your regular season successes or failures. It's a level playing field. Everybody's 0-0. So, put your work record behind you. You've just removed your Popeye the Sailor hat and donned the admiral hat. It's a whole new deal.

Who cares if you were sales person of the month six straight months and set all new sales records?

Weren't *you* the one that designed and coded a custom accounting program that saved the company thousands? Big woop.

But (whine) you were the genius who developed the shipping process that revolutionized the department and helped win dozens of new accounts! Meh.

From this point forward, you'll be cheered or jeered, honored or hated, promoted or demoted based on how you lead your team.

Chances are you've seen episodes of **The Apprentice**, Donald Trump's reality game show where leadership candidates in Trump's empire are downsized one-by-one until the final apprentice wins a "dream job" (read 'nightmare') as a Trump company executive (read 'peon').

Nearly every episode the *leader* (project manager) of the losing team gets fired. And while the whole team faces "the Donald's" wrath, it is rare that Trump fires a rank and file team member. If you're the manager and your team lost, it must be your fault. Trump pulls out "the Cobra," aims it at his victim, and with pursed little billionaire lips utters the phrase, "You're fired." Everyone then just sits there for 27 minutes so the cameras can get a good look at all of their bored reactions. The loser, packed bags in hand, is shamefully whisked away in a cab to an agent where he or she signs a book deal and begins a speaking tour.

The *winning* team's leader, on the other hand, gets praise dumped on him or her and the ultimate weekly prize of immunity from being fired on the next show. Not to mention the whole winning team gets some kind of reward. It might be a dazzling night on Broadway accompanied by some faux-celebrity friend of Trump or a weekend in the Hamptons. Or possibly an evening with Trump's hairdresser. It varies, really, from week to week.

> *"Have fun. Life is very fragile and success doesn't change that. Anything can change without warning. That's why I try not to take any of what's happened too seriously."*
> Donald Trump

Point is, there's a lot of pressure on the *leader*. They're either whooshed away with their team to enjoy the spoils of victory and immunity for another week, or unceremoniously sacked in front of millions of people. It doesn't matter how great they've been the last several episodes as mere team players. "Billy Joe" might have proven himself an invaluable piece of the team puzzle--really delivering--but none of that matters if he can't lead the team three feet in any direction.

It's the same in the business world, isn't it? Sure, the rewards are greater when you're promoted to director or manager, but the risks and responsibilities rise commensurately. The key in leading a team to dizzying heights of success is the ability to delegate. "Delegate or Die" was a favorite phrase by a leader for whom I once worked. He understood that his job was simply to get us to do ours. Sounds simple. If we bought in to some organizational strategy and direction and really pounded out our work, we would enjoy success and he—the boss—would reap great rewards.

So here's the bottom line: Your job is to get them to do their job. What place does levity and humor have—if any—in accomplishing that?

From *They Who Laugh, Last!* Dr. Paul McGhee offers this insight:

"Tom Peters has long had his finger on the pulse of American business. He is now convinced that every company can boost its creativity, team spirit and productivity by building more humor and a lighter style of collegial interaction into the workplace.

"Herb Kelleher is probably the best-known example of a CEO (Southwest Airlines) who insists on hiring employees with a good sense of humor. In filling any position, says Kelleher, 'What we are looking for, first and foremost, is a sense of humor . . . We don't care much about education and expertise, because we can train people... We hire attitudes.'

"In fact, during job interviews, job candidates are specifically asked to give an example of how they've recently used their sense of humor on the job, and how they've 'used humor to defuse a difficult situation.' This approach has helped make Southwest Airlines the most successful airline in the country. Employees love working for Southwest, and do whatever it takes to sustain high levels of performance and quality service. And they have fun in the process! If it works for Southwest, it can also work for you."

Simply telling employees in meetings or memos what you want them to do and how you want it done, doesn't guarantee that they're even listening to you, much less that they're going to do anything. General George S. Patton said, **"Leadership is the art of getting someone else to do something you want done because he wants to do it."**

I think that sums it up nicely. Leadership is an art. We learn from early on that artists are born not created. An artistic bent is an inherent quality, not something learned from books, papers, or distance instructors. How does one truly become a leader and not just a great employee that got promoted? Here's another beauty from our buddy General Patton, **"Don't tell people how to do things, tell them what to do and let them surprise you with their results."**

Ok, so empower your people. Tell them what you want them to do, then stand back and let them go nutty. But again, why should they care about what you want them to do? Will they do it because they fear you or because they respect and "love" you?

Niccolo Macchiavelli, the Renaissance-era philosopher, averred that, **"It's better to be feared than loved, if you cannot have both."** Some leaders have been heard to say, " I don't care if they hate me as long as they respect me," concluding that respect and/or fear are strong motivators for results. How often does the following scenario play out in your workplace?

Milton and Lois are sipping their morning coffee as they walk astride down the 3rd floor corridor at Frigsten's.

Milton: Ugh! I can't stand Ed. The very thought of him turns my stomach.

Lois: (agreeing) Absolutely hate his guts.

Milton: Seriously, I just flat out despise his existence.

Lois: He is a turd of the highest order. A real pile. Icch.

Milton: But you know, you gotta respect him.

Lois: Oh yeah, no doubt. Totally respect him. I'd do anything for him.

Milton: Me too, hands down. But I still hate him.

Lois: Can't even breathe for the hatred!

Where hatred and resentment exist, forget about respect. And without respect there is no way people are really engaged and performing at high levels. Are they doing just enough? Maybe. Are you ok with that? If you are it's because you're not really engaged in your work either. Maybe *your* leader is lacking in the necessaries.

Respect breeds loyalty, which breeds productivity. Perhaps the quickest route to gaining respect is to respect others. Gee, sounds a little like the golden rule, doesn't it? If all of this seems somehow familiar and instinctive, it's because you already know and understand it. You've known this stuff since you were but a toddler. Adrian Gostick and Chester Elton in their book **Managing with Carrots** say that most of today's managers and supervisors could benefit from remembering the things Mom taught them growing up. The golden rule, your 'Ps and Qs,' don't run with a sharpened hatchet, all that good "life" advice your Mom gave you.

Perhaps it's significant to note that **Parenting** magazine found 67% of North American workers say that their moms could do a better job than their bosses running the company. Now, I'm not suggesting that we employ all of mom's home teachings in the workplace. That one about wearing fresh underwear is nobody's business but mine. And if my boss ever called me by my first, middle, and last name while ominously waving a paddle with holes, I'd be tendering my letter of resignation quicker than a six-legged lizard.

But maybe what these survey respondents—and by statistical extension, your employees—are saying is that it doesn't take a multi-degreed genius to just lighten up and lead. "Mom" is the embodiment of security, warmth, trust, respect, peace, etc. She knew that your behavioral slip-ups, accidents, mistakes and lousy GPA should be kept in perspective. Twinkling eyes and rosy cheeks accompanied even the severest of scolding, scolding that was soon after followed up by a greater measure of love.

Was your Mom a great leader? Mine was. Without the aid of a husband she led four children to college degrees, families of their own, and stable, even prosperous, existences. She had to be "both a mother and a father" to us. She ruled with an iron fist and a wooden broom. She worked multiple jobs while furthering her own education. She gave us the freedom to learn for ourselves while providing just enough restriction to keep us from real harm. She actively raised us as church-going, God-loving people, and it stuck.

And amid the crush of the world and its many burdens, she met life's challenges with an irrepressible sense of humor and fun. She found the time—somewhere—to take us bowling, swimming, and on picnics. She taught me how to play tennis. We set up a makeshift ping pong table with a sheet of plywood balanced on top of our small dinner table. I read my first Woody Allen book in 6ᵗʰ grade; she recommended it to me, calling it hilarious. We spent hours playing board and card games as a family.

One evening in 1976 she took me to a movie she wanted me to see because 'she knew I'd love it.' (I jumped from my seat and yelled the name "Rocky! Rocky!" in unison with many of the other theater-goers during the climactic final round.) She woke us all up late one school night to watch a Mohammed Ali fight on TV, because "this is the greatest fighter ever, and I want you kids to see him."

Her quick wit and oft times raucous laughter were legendary among our friends and extended family, but she didn't have a reputation as a "comic." She didn't really tell jokes so much as she related humorous stories and anecdotes. She simply understood what Charlie Chaplin once said, "A day without laughter is a day wasted."

Now, I'm not suggesting that just because *your* mother exhibited BrowKnitter or even JawClencher tendencies she was a bad family leader. Just because you can't recall ever actually seeing your mother crack a smile or tell a joke or funny story doesn't mean she did a bad job. The fact is you loved your mom even if she was a sour-puss tyrant. (Let's be real, there aren't many of those moms left anyway.)

But if she could have lightened up just a bit, let her tightly wound hair bun down now and then and had some fun, your memories of her would be fuller and richer. And as a child you likely would have been quicker and more willing to please her with good behavior and hard work. Why? Because it's easier to work hard for someone that you know respects and cares for you. A smiling countenance, shining eyes, a little laugh or even a gregarious, hearty laugh is an easily read indication that you are loved. Good moms have a *sense* of humor.

> *If I had no sense of humor, I would long ago*
> *have committed suicide.*
> *Mahatma Gandhi*

A truly great leader will display the same *sense* of humor that moms do, the uncanny perspective that it's all right to cut loose every now and then, to "take a chill pill" and stop furrowing the brow. As kids, we're simply more likely to positively respond to a command from a loving and gentle parent than from the other kind. Can you become the corporate equivalent of somebody's Mommy? If 2/3 of your people are saying you'd take a distant 2nd place behind their mothers for Best Boss, then you'd better discover what 9 out of 10 mothers know instinctively: **lead with levity**.

According to management professor David Abramis, when supervisors encourage appropriate playfulness at work and show their own sense of humor in a good-natured way, they motivate better productivity, job satisfaction, morale, creativity, and teamwork.

Business philosopher Jim Rohn believes there are six qualities of skilled leaders and one of them is, "Develop humor without folly. That's important for a leader. In leadership, we learn that it's okay to be witty, but not silly. It's okay to be fun, but not foolish."

It's all about your credibility as a leader. The great ones know that they can't lead with levity *only*; they must establish a bedrock of credibility first. A well-rounded manager that has a solid business vision and commitment to company goals is more qualified to bring mirth into the mix because he or she has already established credibility. The joker/leader who kills 'em in the cafeteria but can't bring it in the boardroom will ultimately lose loyalty.

Years ago I auditioned to be an on-air host for QVC. It was an open call audition at the company's headquarters in West Chester, PA. Hundreds of East coast news reporters and actors turned out to take a shot. I happened to be in Washington, D.C. on business and I took the opportunity as well.

After a four or five hour wait it was finally my turn. I was given about two minutes to "sell" whatever I wanted to a couple of producers. I chose to pitch the small video camera I had in my bag. I figured I'd play to my strengths: I'm a guy and I love electronics. Plus I knew I could leverage my somewhat witty personality and ability to ad-lib some comedy. I began my spiel and noticed them lean forward with renewed interest in their tedious task.

Two weeks later I got a call from an assistant who told me that I was being invited back to another audition. He said only 10 were chosen to return, nine women and me. This time they flew me back on their dime. Long story short, I didn't get hired. After a day of on-camera tests and ad-libbing about gardening tools and luggage, they came to the conclusion that while they *loved* my levity they were afraid it would cast aspersions on my credibility as a salesman.

And they were right.

I didn't know jack about jewelry. Or power tools for that matter. So, all I had to fall back on was "being casual, kicking back and having fun," which is great, but only as as an outward expression of an inner credibility. That credibility I did not possess.

GreatLeaders will establish themselves as someone who belongs in that position, someone who deserves the at-times affectionate title of "boss." Then levity will lead to loyalty.

LEADING WITH LEVITY THROUGHOUT HISTORY

President Abraham Lincoln had a particular General who liked to send dispatches that were always headed: "Headquarters in the Saddle." And everyday, or every other day, Lincoln would get one of these messages entitled "Headquarters in the Saddle." And he got quite annoyed with this, but he kept quiet, as he normally did, until, finally, one day somebody asked him about this General and about this habit of heading all these dispatches "Headquarters in the Saddle." And Lincoln said, "It seems to me that the General has his headquarters where his hindquarters ought to be."

On another occasion, he was confronted by a group of Washington officials who were complaining about General Grant and the fact that there was a rumor going around that General Grant was a regular drinker of alcoholic beverages. And Lincoln replied, "By the way, can you tell me where he gets his whiskey? He has given us successes, and if his whiskey does it, I should like to send a barrel of the same to every General in the field."

Lincoln once interrupted a meeting by reading an amusing story with the hope of dispelling the black clouds hovering over his staff. But no one as much as smiled. Finally, Lincoln said, "Gentlemen, why don't you laugh? With the fearful strain that is upon me day and night, if I did not laugh I should die, and you need this medicine as much as I do."

Governor Granholm of the State of Michigan proclaimed May 4, 2003 as World Laughter Day in Michigan. In the official proclamation the governor wrote:

Whereas, Laughter is a free and natural expression of the joyful human spirit and promotes good health, improves morale and increases productivity at work, facilitates the healing of illness, melts away stress, works wonders to help students in the classroom, is a hallmark of a healthy family life, and promotes widespread harmony; and

Whereas, On World Laughter Day, all citizens are encouraged and invited to set their cares and differences aside and engage in good-hearted acts of laughing out loud, smiles, silliness, giggles, clowning, chuckles, guffaws, titters, grins and happy foolishness in the spirit of health, peace and joy...

Governor Jennifer Granholm, *mother* of three, gets it.

CHAPTER 3

A Sense of Humor Is Just That

Our five senses are incomplete without the sixth—a sense of humor.
Author unknown

For some reason many of us have arrived at the conclusion that if somebody has a "good sense of humor" it means they're "funny." If you have a good sense of direction does that make you a good driver? If you have a good sense of logic does that make you a Vulcan? And though someone may do something that is funny that doesn't always equate with a sense of humor. If someone makes you laugh, does that automatically qualify him or her as possessor of said sense?

Humor doesn't always evoke laughter. Does something have to be funny for you to laugh at it? Certainly people laugh at things that aren't funny. I once actually laughed watching an ABC sitcom, if you can believe it. Developing and applying humor in the workplace strikes its intended targets in diverse ways. Some guffaw. Others chortle. Snicker. Giggle. Chuckle. Blow milk from their nostrils. Wet themselves. You get the idea.

> *The sense of humor has other things*
> *to do than to make itself conspicuous*
> *in the act of laughter.*
> *Alice Meynell*

There is no bit of mirth that strikes two people exactly the same way. Your friend is reading an article in the newspaper and laughing uncontrollably. Your curiosity piqued, you grab the paper with a smile of anticipation for the therapy this good laugh will give you. You read the joke/cartoon/editorial and your reaction is far less dramatic than that of your friend. You nod and smile and politely say, "Hmm. That's funny." Meanwhile your friend is hooking up to an oxygen tank.

The old "I guess you had to be there" axiom supports the fundamental truth that funny is relative. So even having a *sense* of humor is based on what *you* believe is humorous or amusing. Let's face it: there is no international standard of humor weights and measures. Nobody can tell you what is funny. They can only tell you what *they* think is funny.

Thank heavens there is no **Laugh Enforcement Department**. I can just see "Laugh Cops" breaking down my door and hauling me away in cuffs because I found last night's Tonight Show monologue a complete waste of time.

"We understand you didn't care for the President Bush bit," they'll say.

"No. I didn't."

"Stop squirming, the cuffs won't hurt. You didn't laugh at all?"

"There was nothing funny about it."

"Not funny, huh? Why don't you make this easy on yourself?" they say as they reach for the nightstick.

"I'm sorry, but it was a lame bit." I am thwacked on the skull.

At this point a half dozen laughter swat troopers swing in through the windows and taser me for good measure. A bystander with a camcorder rolling catches one of them throwing a pie in my face. Another squirts water in my eye from his badge.

The point is nobody can tell you that because you don't make people laugh or that you didn't howl at a joke, you don't have a sense of humor.

Bad guys in movies and TV shows are always laughing about something. And while a hearty laugh is certainly good for the stressful lifestyle of your average criminal psychopath, I doubt that I would find anything truly humorous about torturing to death some well-meaning super spy. On the other hand maybe I "had to be there."

Lawrence J. Peter and Bill Dana, in their book *The Laughter Prescription*, say, "Realize that a sense of humor is deeper than laughter, more satisfying than comedy, and delivers more rewards than merely being entertaining. A sense of humor sees the fun in everyday experiences. *It is more important to have fun than it is to be funny.*"

Especially when your material tanks. Let's face it, if you're only in this for the laughs you're in for some serious slams to your self-esteem. For the average non-comedian, not only is it "more important to have fun than it is to be funny," it's also a heck of a lot easier.

If you can somehow develop a true *sense* of humor and not worry about just being funny, you'll be miles ahead of other managers who force comedy on an unwilling/unsuspecting audience.

> *A sense of humor is part of the art of leadership, of getting along with people, of getting things done.*
> Dwight D. Eisenhower

In case you're a bit rusty on your history, Dwight D. Eisenhower was a pretty famous World War II general. He helped lead the allied forces on to enormous successes. He was honored, revered, respected and loved. If memory serves, he became the CEO of this world's mightiest nation. He fought, charged, attacked, strategized, and killed. And here he is telling us that humor is part of the art of leadership. Now, I don't imagine he was necessarily doing shtick while crouched in a foxhole or atop a tank ("Winston Churchill walks into a bar…"), but evidently he was convinced of the power of levity: "getting along with people…getting things done."

Leaders that discover their sense of humor and wield it frequently have typically developed other critical leadership senses. A sense of humor isn't just something you have; it isn't your best quality or something you turn on and off. It *is you*. By the same token, a great leader also exhibits a sense of fairness, a sense of mercy, a sense of judgment, a sense of compassion. These senses, too, make up who they *are*; they're not merely a laundry list of available traits to draw on when circumstances require. Leaders that truly care about their people and not merely what their people do, will discover that a sense of humor is fundamental to their overall success.

Legendary leader Pete Harman, the first and largest franchisee of Kentucky Fried Chicken espoused the idea that he's not in the chicken business, he's in the people business. His mission, as he sees it, is to simply enable other people to get ahead, to have retirement and savings, to live fulfilling lives. In fact Harman devised his own profit-sharing program for all employees decades before similar programs became popular.

Harman's leadership philosophy has always been grounded in respect for individuals. "Be around your people a lot," he said in *Secret Recipe, Pete Harman, The Man Behind the Bucket*. "Let them know daily how you feel." Harman was known to visit his restaurants every day and greet employees personally, often putting a caring arm around their shoulders.

At Harman Management Corp, Pete's HQ for his chain of 350 franchises, one of their core values is "fun." Harman is a leader who innately understands how to treat his people right. It's not that he's a "card" or a "cutup" or a great joketeller. If he were, Pete Harman might have ruled the universe. Still he had his moments.

In 1957 he helped out a fellow restaurateur in Colorado who had purchased 500 thick paper buckets but didn't know what to do with them. At the request of Harman's friend and partner Harland (Colonel) Sanders, Harman took the buckets off the man's hands and put them to use. He said, "We need to sell larger orders to build the business. Let's put fourteen pieces in this bucket and make it a new menu item that will feed a family of five."

At the time, the Harman restaurants were offering a dinner box with three pieces of chicken in it. Pete wanted to offer five rolls with the new dinner and to improve the bucket's heft at the same time. Even with the rolls added, he wasn't happy with how the bucket felt. "This doesn't weigh enough. It doesn't feel like $3.50." So he dumped the chicken out and stuck a pint of gravy in the bottom then put the chicken around it.

"What if they dump this thing out and the gravy spills?" Pete was asked.

"Oh, hell, they'll figure it out. But now it feels like $3.50," he responded.

It's a cute story, isn't it? It elicits a chuckle. And it beautifully illustrates Harman's *sense* of humor. Though he set up no rehearsed joke or riddle, he still delivered a very natural and timely punch line. By the way, were you offended by his using 'h-e-double hockey sticks'? While Harman is a religious man, he understood the humor of the moment, without overstepping total propriety. Leaders with levity manage to find a balance, some moderation in their mirth.

So, how do you do it? The truth is everyone has an innate sense of humor. No single human exists without some inclination to jest and levity. But beyond the joke, the gag, the bit, the insult, etc. a sense of humor—*your* sense of humor—is a matter of attitude, not timing and tone. It's how you carry yourself. How you react to everyday situations. It's in your conversations with co-workers and subordinates. I daresay you might go an entire day, a week, a month, a decade!—without telling a single "joke" and still have a remarkable and possibly legendary sense of humor.

And your people will love you. Why? You put them at ease. They can relax around you. The stress and demands of business don't automatically dissipate, but a lot of the pressure does. And when they love (honor/respect/revere) you, imagine the lengths they'll go to for you. A wise man once said, "Serve those you love, and love those you serve."

You already possess the gift of humor. Understand, humor goes both ways. It's a lot like holiday gifts. You either give or receive. Sometimes both. Same thing with levity. You're not always the giver. Just kick back and enjoy someone else's wit. Boom. There's your sense of humor. It's in there. You just need to power it up.

Universal Truth # 1: Your employees fear you, just as you fear your superior. You are the master of all that is good or bad about their existence. Peace, joy, satisfaction, security…in your people's eyes you control all of those things. And while fear can motivate a form of productivity and accomplishment, it likely won't be an employee's best work.

> *It is better to be feared than loved, if you cannot be both.*
> *Niccolo Machiavelli*

> *Niccolo Machiavelli was a lonely leader.*
> *Scott Christopher*

Universal Truth # 2: Your employees *hate* and fear you. But only if you're a JawClenching, BrowKnitter that subscribes to Machiavellian ideas. If you can work an occasional twinkle in your eyes, they'll still fear you, but the loathing subsides.

Universal Truth # 3: Having a sense of humor will not destroy your credibility. Just because you display signs of levity and playfulness doesn't mean you're a mouth-breathing, uneducated pushover. Quite the opposite is true. A good sense of humor actually can enhance your credibility.

Universal Truth # 4: Your people will be a hundred times more likely to follow you and produce for you if you can simply lighten up a titch. What is a titch? A scosh.

Lighten up. Laugh a little. Loosen your top button. Smile. I'm not talking about becoming Will Farrell. I'm talking about becoming Will Marriott. Here's what he said in 1964, *"It's important to listen to employees, ask questions of them, say 'Good Morning' to them, ask about their families, and get to know a little bit about their aspirations, ambitions, home life and work motivations."*

That's pretty sound, practical advice from a leader who's taken his professional career pretty far. Can you do it? Set a goal for yourself that tomorrow you're going to say 'good morning' to five people and ask about their families. Write it down and do it. A goal not written is but a wish, right? And remember to smile when you do it. The grumpy, perfunctory "Mornin.' Family good?" as you pass in the break room won't knock anyone dead.

The whole idea behind levity, mirth, humor and playfulness is to instill a sense of ease and security among your people. It's not about having the sharpest wit or the greatest punch line, so go easy on yourself. Forget about being the next Robin Williams and focus instead on being the next Robin Gibb (the BeeGees) who, in 1976, said,

"Whatcha doin on your back? Ahh.
Whatcha doin on your back? Ahh.

You should be dancin', yeah.
Dancin', yeah."

See? He just wants you to get out there, sing chipmunk falsetto, and enjoy 'whatcha do.' (True, the toothy Gibb brothers aren't exactly a case study in organizational leadership, but they led us to the dance floor and Barry had great hair.) There's no need for elaborate, complicated, and time-consuming jokes. Just loosen your tie a little, and as British rocker Ian Brodie sang, "Crack up your face and give us a smile."

LEADING WITH LEVITY THROUGHOUT HISTORY

Alexander the Great, while leading his army to victories throughout Persia, Asia Minor, Egypt, and Arabia, promised his workforce loads of gold and war booty. Having collected an enormous amount of gold from his many conquests, Al promised to pay all of his soldiers' debts. Using the honor system, he allowed his men to come and take from his personal pile whatever they needed to satisfy their debtors. By day's end they had taken 500 tons of gold. Yes, 500 TONS of gold. After unleashing a "d'oh!" that could be heard from as far off as Athens, Alexander the Great cracked a smile, shook his head and said, "Well, I've got my health." He died of the flu days later.

CHAPTER 4

Discovering Your Levity

This above all; to thine own self be true.
William Shakespeare

"I wish I was more like Johnson in sales. He's so funny. Maybe I should try to be more like him."

Imitation *is* the most sincere form of flattery but not if Johnson is a wannabe Jim Carrey type and you "flatter" him by opening a meeting throwing your voice out of your rear. Although it is certainly beneficial to observe what others do to make people laugh, stick to what you know, or rather who you know: You.

You're not going to have to change much of what you're already doing (unless you're a public nose-picker.) The trouble comes when you try to make a quantum leap into being one hundred percent funny. Not only will it burn you out, your employees will see right though it.

One of my favorite film comedies is "What about Bob?" starring Bill Murray. If you've seen it you'll remember that Murray's paranoid, delusional, multi-phobic Bob had to take "baby steps" to overcome his problems. "Baby steps across the room. Baby steps to the elevator," he would mutter to himself.

It's the same with you and finding your comic voice or persona. Within reason, it's okay to cannibalize bits and pieces from other people, but pace yourself. You cannot simply wholesale assume the personality of somebody funny.

I remember starting out as a young stand-up comic. I always wrote my own material and put my own spin on things. At one time in my hunger to expand my routine I tried some material that I'd heard from another comic. Here's a shocker: It didn't work. I wasn't being myself. I was trying to be someone else. Humor done right is personal because it originates from your own experience.

Ask yourself: What makes me laugh?

Though laughter isn't always the desired or necessary outcome of good humor (in another chapter we'll discuss the benefits of laughter), nor concrete evidence that something is truly funny, it's a reasonable place to begin. So think about it. What makes you laugh?

And I mean really laugh. Hard. The sore stomach type. Has anything ever got you *screaming* with laughter, where you have said in a strained, falsetto voice, "I can't breathe. I can't breathe. I ca- bree-. BAAAAAAAAAAAhahahahahahaha!?" Sadly, you may have to think way back to when you were a flatulent teenager or a carefree kid to remember an outburst like this.

If you've never experienced this level of oxygen deprivation before, if you've never enjoyed the afterglow of a laughter-driven "ab" workout, if you've never once lost the motor skills needed to stay vertical (while sober) and actually fallen to the earth in a heaving fit of cackles...you might be a redneck. Hang on, that's not right.

Ok, then, what makes you grin? Or simply moves you to muse, "That's funny," even though you may not be laughing. In order for you to discover your own sense of humor, it's a good idea to expose yourself to some universally accepted funny material; i.e., things that make *others* laugh.

Take a look at the American Film Institute's list of the Top 100 American Comedies. Sure, it's just a bunch of movie industry types—and who cares what they think, right?—but at least they found the time in their busy schedules (hiring house help and slumming in Park City) to vote on and compile a list. As you read through these, think about the breadth of comedy represented. Clearly, not all comedies are created equal, at least by the AFI's definition. Mark the ones that made you laugh. Mark those that didn't make you laugh, but you thought were funny anyway. My own comments are included, where applicable (if I saw the film), thus you can even compare your *sense* of humor with mine.

1. SOME LIKE IT HOT (1959)—You've GOT to be kidding me. Number one of all time? Great movie. Lemmon and Curtis, and Marilyn. A few small chuckles. But number one?

2. TOOTSIE (1982)—Another "drag" movie. That's two in the top two. The funniest person in this movie is Bill Murray. Now he made me laugh. Nearly always does.

3. DR. STRANGELOVE OR: HOW I LEARNED TO STOP WORRYING AND LOVE THE BOMB (1964)—Sorry. I don't recall laughing much. Slim Pickens riding a missile was about it for me.

4. ANNIE HALL (1977)—Some great belly laughs for me, but then I am a Woody fan.

5. DUCK SOUP (1933)—Old school genius. The "mirror" scene is not only a true comedy classic, but it still makes me howl. My five sons and I own this video; they love Harpo. We all sit and laugh together.

6. BLAZING SADDLES (1974)—Gene Wilder makes me laugh just seeing him in my head. Harvey Korman does the same.

7. M*A*S*H (1970)—The TV show evoked some real laughs for me. The movie, not so much.

8. IT HAPPENED ONE NIGHT (1934)—Amusing and cute. One of the first romantic comedies. But I don't recall laughing.

9. THE GRADUATE (1967)—One of the all-time great movies, and a personal top ten choice. Not terribly funny, though.

10. AIRPLANE! (1980)—Non-stop gags and bits don't always make me laugh. Fun to watch, though.

11. THE PRODUCERS (1968)—Another great Gene Wilder performance.

12. A NIGHT AT THE OPERA (1935)—A few laughs, but nothing like Duck Soup for me.

13. YOUNG FRANKENSTEIN (1974)—Gene Wilder and an all-star cast of comics. Wildly entertaining, but I wasn't slapping my knee.

14. BRINGING UP BABY (1938)

15. THE PHILADELPHIA STORY (1940)

16. SINGIN' IN THE RAIN (1952)

17. THE ODD COUPLE (1968)—Neil Simon's brilliant dialogue perfectly delivered by Lemmon and Matthau equals lots of laughs.

18. THE GENERAL (1927)

19. HIS GIRL FRIDAY (1940)

20. THE APARTMENT (1960)

21. A FISH CALLED WANDA (1988)—Non-stop comedy. John Cleese nearly always makes me laugh out loud.

22. ADAM'S RIB (1949)

23. WHEN HARRY MET SALLY... (1989)—Amusing. Cute. No real gut-busters. Even the famous diner scene. Bruno Kirby and Billy Crystal had some good moments, but then, they usually do.

24. BORN YESTERDAY (1950)

25. THE GOLD RUSH (1925)

26. BEING THERE (1979)—Sellars is brilliant, but hardly a laugher.

27. THERE'S SOMETHING ABOUT MARY (1998)—The only Ben Stiller film on the list. Shame.

28. GHOSTBUSTERS (1984)—Out loud laughs, mostly because of Bill Murray.

29. THIS IS SPINAL TAP (1984)—Five-star laugher. If you haven't seen this 'Father of Mockumentaries,' you haven't lived. This is one of those movies where I was laughing throughout, but my friend fell asleep early on. If you just don't get it, it's ok. Remember, humor is unique to you.

30. ARSENIC AND OLD LACE (1944)

31. RAISING ARIZONA (1987)—Absolutely hilarious, and like Spinal Tap, abundantly quotable.

32. THE THIN MAN (1934)

33. MODERN TIMES (1936)

34. GROUNDHOG DAY (1993)—"Oh, you speak French?" Andie MacDowell asks. "Oui," Bill Murray quietly replies. I'm laughing just thinking about it.

35. HARVEY (1950)

36. NATIONAL LAMPOON'S ANIMAL HOUSE (1978)—Entertaining and marginally funny. Lamentably, the father of all the crude, sophomoric, teen sex and party movies

to follow. This was the only one that had any truly funny moments, however.

37. THE GREAT DICTATOR (1940)

38. CITY LIGHTS (1931)

39. SULLIVAN'S TRAVELS (1941)

40. IT'S A MAD MAD MAD MAD WORLD (1963)—"I'm coming for you Momma. You're baby's coming to save you, Momma!" Dick Shawn's sobbing hipster makes my boys and me wheeze with laughter.

41. MOONSTRUCK (1987)—Meh.

42. BIG (1988)—Sweet movie. Amusing.

43. AMERICAN GRAFFITI (1973)—A few really good laughs, particularly from Terry the (Tiger) Toad.

44. MY MAN GODFREY (1936)

45. HAROLD AND MAUDE (1972)

46. MANHATTAN (1979)—Sorry, but the Woodman makes me cackle. The hair, the glasses, the wimp...together with the witty dialogue. Kills me.

47. SHAMPOO (1975)

48. A SHOT IN THE DARK (1964)—Peter Sellars' first go as Clouseau. More subtle than later Pink Panther films. A few great laughs.

49. TO BE OR NOT TO BE (1942)

50. CAT BALLOU (1965)

51. THE SEVEN YEAR ITCH (1955)

52. NINOTCHKA (1939)

53. ARTHUR (1981)—Just his cackling, drunken laugh makes me smile. "Where is the rest of this moose?"

54. THE MIRACLE OF MORGAN'S CREEK (1944)

55. THE LADY EVE (1941)

56. ABBOTT AND COSTELLO MEET FRANKENSTEIN (1948)—It wasn't till I was an adult that I realized what a great straight man Bud Abbott was. And of course Costello can always make me laugh.

57. DINER (1982)

58. IT'S A GIFT (1934)

59. A DAY AT THE RACES (1937)—More Groucho and bros.

60. TOPPER (1937)

61. WHAT'S UP, DOC? (1972)—Classic comedy. Very funny. Madeline Kahn is in a lot of these movies, isn't she?

62. SHERLOCK, JR. (1924)

63. BEVERLY HILLS COP (1984)—There was a time when Eddie Murphy could do no wrong. Good action movie with really good laughs.

64. BROADCAST NEWS (1987)—Anything Albert Brooks does gives me genuine laughs.

65. HORSE FEATHERS (1932)—Yet another Marx Brothers. Ok, already. Let's leave a little room for a Jim Carrey or Steve Martin movie.

66. TAKE THE MONEY AND RUN (1969)—Another very funny Woody movie. Laughed a lot, as usual.

67. MRS. DOUBTFIRE (1993)—One of those amusing films coupled with a few hearty laughs

68. THE AWFUL TRUTH (1937)

69. BANANAS (1971)—More good Woody laughs. Some that induce incontinence.

70. MR. DEEDS GOES TO TOWN (1936)—I know this isn't the Adam Sandler one, but his version actually made me laugh.

71. CADDYSHACK (1980)—I know Murray's "Carl" is everybody's favorite quotable character, but honestly it's not anywhere near as funny as some of his other stuff. In fact, it's not even the funniest in this movie. Rodney Dangerfield and Ted Knight make me laugh most.

72. MR. BLANDINGS BUILDS HIS DREAM HOUSE (1948)— This doesn't even *sound* funny.

73. MONKEY BUSINESS (1931)

74. 9 TO 5 (1980)—Dabney Coleman got me really laughing.

75. SHE DONE HIM WRONG (1933)

76. VICTOR/VICTORIA (1982)

77. THE PALM BEACH STORY (1942)

78. ROAD TO MOROCCO (1942)

79. THE FRESHMAN (1925)

80. SLEEPER (1973)—More Woody. I love the guy, but come on. No "Ace Ventura" or "Dumb and Dumber?"

81. THE NAVIGATOR (1924)

82. PRIVATE BENJAMIN (1980)

83. FATHER OF THE BRIDE (1950)—Blew the chance to do Steve Martin justice; the updated version with Martin Short was hilarious .

84. LOST IN AMERICA (1985)—If you don't get Albert Brooks, see this movie. He absolutely will make you laugh. And if not, call me, and I'll refund your money.

85. DINNER AT EIGHT (1933)

86. CITY SLICKERS (1991)—If Crystal, Kirby, and Daniel Stern don't get you laughing, check your pulse because you're dead. But hey, that's just me.

87. FAST TIMES AT RIDGEMONT HIGH (1982)—Sure it's a classic and it launched a bunch of careers. But, except for a few Sean Penn chuckles, it's not a great comedy.

88. BEETLEJUICE (1988)—Michael Keaton's good for a few laughs—he was much funnier in Ron Howard's Nightshift.

89. THE JERK (1979)—Well, well. It's a Steve Martin movie. Old school Steve is still funny.

90. WOMAN OF THE YEAR (1942)

91. THE HEARTBREAK KID (1972)—Charles Grodin used to kill me on Carson and Letterman.

92. BALL OF FIRE (1941)

93. FARGO (1996)—Witty, smart and amusing. Few real laughs for me though.

94. AUNTIE MAME (1958)

95. SILVER STREAK (1976)—Gene Wilder consistently made me laugh in the 70s.

96. SONS OF THE DESERT (1933)

97. BULL DURHAM (1988)—Meh.

98. THE COURT JESTER (1956)

99. THE NUTTY PROFESSOR (1963)—Jerry Lewis at the height of his game. His Buddy Love is still better than Eddie Murphy's, but Murphy's version—particularly the dinner scene where he plays nearly every family member—delivered more laughs.

100. GOOD MORNING, VIETNAM (1987)—Vintage frenetic, loose-cannon Williams with pursuant laughs.

So, how'd you do? How many of the top 100 truly make you laugh? I counted 33. For my money, Adam Sandler, Jim Carrey, Mike Myers, Eddie Murphy, Ben Stiller and other contemporary comic actors deserve a spot or two on there. While I'm the first to admit that the majority of their kind of work is sophomoric and low-brow, I must confess that some of the biggest laughs come from their films as well.

Owen Wilson makes me howl with laughter, while others find him annoying. Case in point: The locker room interview scene in *Starsky and Hutch*. Wilson and Stiller are questioning a cheerleader. Wilson's excited nervousness and dropped-jaw reactions as she changes clothes absolutely killed me. I laughed loud and long (and it really felt good), yet no other soul in the theater was even chortling. I must have sounded like I was kidding, the way I was carrying on. I teetered on the edge of judging the other audience members as humorless cretins, but reminded myself that humor is relative to each person.

Look back over the list and see how often you agree with my assessments. Chances are good that we'll gel on a few, but while I'm slapping my knee over the following Woody Allen moment from **Manhattan**, you may not even think it amusing:

Diane Keaton: *I thought you wanted to kiss me that day at the planetarium.*

Woody: *I did. You were soaking wet from the rain and I had a mad impulse to throw you down on the lunar surface and commit interstellar perversions with you.*

Six steps to discovering your own sense of humor.

1-Learn

What is humor? Why should you care? What kind of humor is available to you as a seeker of a sense of it? Go to Wikipedia.com and search "humor" in English. Read every word of that article, and follow the links. You'll learn all you need to know about the origin, techniques and styles of humor in short order. Metaphor, timing, hyperbole, verbal, non-verbal, wordplay, slapstick, sarcasm...every flavor of humor is defined. Learn the theory of humor.

2-Exposure

Reading humorous materials has a much greater impact than merely passively observing. Reading is active and requires effort and brainpower. You have ample time to process and dissect humor when reading. Make books and articles your number one source of comic exposure. The printed word captures subtle styles of humor. Alliteration, puns, wordplay, sarcasm are more easily consumed and digested.

Next time you're killing a few hours at Border's check out the humor section. Buy the latest Dave Barry and don't sleep till you've finished it. I guarantee it'll awaken something inside you. The Far Side, Calvin and Hobbes, Dilbert and other cartoon collections are favorites for millions of people. Read them. Which ones make you laugh?

Once you've committed to reading something purportedly humorous on a regular basis you can begin catching up on all those AFI comedies you've never seen. Watch one or two a week. Stretch yourself. You have no idea what will get you laughing, right? So, fire up an old black and white classic. Groucho, Bud and Lou, even the Three Stooges. See what all the fuss is about.

What are the top 5 or 10 sitcoms in the Nielsen ratings? Watch them all. Just the title of some of them will turn you off. But give it a shot. Expose yourself to what large groups of regular people consider funny enough to spend a half hour of their lives viewing. Judge for yourself. Do they make you laugh? Are you merely amused? Do you need to schedule an appointment with Dr. Kevorkian?

The bottom line on Exposure is to sample a broad range of what is universally classified as humorous.

3-Value

With massive dosages of exposure to disparate comic material, you'll reach the inevitable phase of wanting to hurl. After deploying an entire roll of Brawny, get down to the business of sorting through your feelings.

What made you laugh out loud? Which book or film at least put a smile on your face? What type of verbal humor will you want to avoid either giving or receiving?

Of the numerous flavors of humor you Learned about and Exposed yourself to, which ones do you Value most? Maybe you appreciate a smattering of all humor, if it's done well. Whatever the case, write it down. Thinking about it, writing it down and reading it will help solidify the ideas. Your "style" starts formulating in the Value phase.

4-Inventory

One of the funniest people I've ever known—Neil Labute, he's a playwright and Hollywood film director—likens a keen wit and sense of humor with a filing cabinet in his head. He says that he is constantly mining humor from different sources; TV, movies, books, life experiences, other people, and then storing away these little comic files in his mental cabinet. When opportunities present themselves, Neil simply accesses the appropriate file and applies its contents.

I've used the same technique for years. If nothing else, it serves as a continual reminder to keep updating the files. Exposure is an ongoing process to develop and refine the content of your sense of humor storage. You'll likely find yourself reserving your files for humor that you truly Value. You won't clutter your inventory or waste precious space for levity that falls outside your Values; you simply will have no use for it.

5-Test

Launch it out there. See what works. If you've followed the first four steps and discovered that you Value and Inventory *jokes*, then pull up a file and let one fly. Prepare for failure, you may not score on your first at-bat. Be thick-skinned and remember you're simply discovering your sense of humor.

Perhaps you realize that you enjoy witty banter and puns. Test your ability to dive in and contribute. An active and frequently updated mental filing system will be crucial. Maybe you only wish to be a spectator, that you're not ready to dive in to the verbal volleys. That's ok, be a receiver. Your people need to see that you appreciate humor, whether or not you create it.

6-Yours

Remember that it's your skin you have to fit in, not somebody else's. This sense of humor you're developing is uniquely yours. The more true you stay to what you honestly think and feel, the more authentic your humor will resonate to others. Be yourself.

A couple of years ago, a young filmmaker named Jared Hess called me and asked if I would be in his film. I knew Jared as an ambitious college student who frequented film sets as a production assistant or grip. I had no idea he aspired to direct.

He told me that his student film was the inspiration for this new feature length film and that the Sundance Film Festival had all but assured him a place in the competition. They were working on very little budget. In fact, if I wanted to do it I would have to drive myself up to Idaho and work for free. It was a small role, one or two lines, hardly worth the effort. I asked him what the title of his film was. **Napoleon Dynamite**, he said. After suppressing a chuckle, I politely declined and wished him all the best.

Do you remember that movie? Of course you do. Not only is that film concrete evidence of the yawning chasm between what you think is funny and what I think is funny, it also supports the notion to be true to who you are. Jared Hess and his wife (who co-wrote) stayed true to their concept of a comedy and it paid off. Little Jared is now a bona fide Hollywood director of films and commercials.

So, the six steps to discovering your sense of humor are:

> **L**earn
> **E**xposure
> **V**alue
> **I**nventory
> **T**est
> **Y**ours

Wow, how bizarre is that, huh? Did you notice the first letter of each word together spell 'levity'? I love when that happens. It's like the planets aligning. Spooky.

CHAPTER 5

A Time and Place

Ecclesiastes 3:4
A time to weep, and a time to [a]__laugh__; a time to [b]<u>mourn</u>, and a time to dance

Comedy really is about timing. But not the timing you normally associate with joke-tellers and standup comics. Carson, Youngman, Groucho, they were masters of comedic timing. The timing you need to master has more to do with understanding when the time is right.

A manager who has learned the subtle art of picking and placing his or her comic moments will reap greater benefits. As a young man I learned from my seniors that just because something occurs to you doesn't mean you have to say it. If it pops into your head, take a second—in some cases a microsecond—and measure it before launching it out there.

In leading with levity, restraint is job one.

A principal has a young man seated in front of him. The man looks sternly at the 7th-grader and asks, "Do you have any idea what you've done?" The boy—blessed with the ability to snap back comical answers—blurts out, "Why? Don't *you* know either? And you call yourself a principal." Now that's funny, but, depending on the principal, the boy will have either diffused a tense situation (unlikely in this case) or guaranteed a permanent place in detention.

Hard to believe there are still those men out there who, when asked by their entrapping wives, "Do these jeans make my butt look big?" still shoot back the hackneyed and obvious, "No. Your fat makes your butt look big."

This is one of those "better left unsaid" examples. Certainly the day-to-day work environment is rife with opportunities to let loose with cynical tirades, witty comebacks, mockery, sarcasm, and parody. And just because those opportunities rise up and present themselves like a mandrill in heat, doesn't mean you have to seize them.

The "Time and Place" principle is the most fundamental law of workplace humor. Time and Place trumps every bit of practical humor advice presented in this book. Every idea, trick, tip, suggestion, and piece of advice mean squattolini where T&P criteria is unmet.

The Time and Place rule is defined as: *The universally ignored law which dictates the likelihood that your efforts at leading with levity will either succeed or fail. Before any workplace humor is executed, its bearer must determine, using *sound judgment, if said humor is appropriate for both the physical setting and the space in time which it occupies.* *Where sound judgment does not exist, the T&P rule means as much as a Milli Vanilli Grammy.

Managing with mirth requires strict adherence to this rule. Unfortunately T&P is almost completely subject to the wisdom and judgment of its followers, and 100% perfect judgment is something we all lack. Let's explain T&P with an example. In fact let's back up a bit to the "wifey got back" scenario.

"Do these jeans make my butt look big?"
"No, your fat makes your butt look big."

Both *time* and *place* violations occurred with the husband's response. There is NEVER a good time nor place for that kind of brutally honest, yet pants-wettingly humorous reply when it is given *directly to the wife*. Sharing this witticism with guys at the gym the next day is another thing. But with the actual wife you will never, ever make a case.

Shower her with diamonds, furs, and credit cards. Make her favorite dinner. Do the dishes. Change a poopy diaper. Tuck her into silk sheets and begin rubbing her feet with warm water and a loofa. Build up that positive emotional bank account till your guts bleed love coins.

Now say, "Your fat makes your butt look big."

Sorry. It will forever remain a No-No. Funny? Oh sure, but again, the only T&P where this little exchange will score laughs is when it is excitedly repeated by someone who *almost* did it. Someone who toed the line, took a deep breath, wrapped his mouth around the words and…bailed. "But I thought about it," he'll proclaim. "I almost did it. And it would have been glorious!"

The Time and Place rule encompasses three key components: Necessity, Impact, and Consequence.

Necessity: Is your comedy called for? Is this a situation where a bit of levity would in some way a) benefit you b) benefit another c) diffuse tension (benefit both) d)enhance existing humor?

When a beautiful punchline has been teed up for you to drive out there like a John Daly screamer, you've got to ask yourself if it's really necessary. Are people expecting it? Hoping for it? Would it be piling on? Maybe appetites for humor are satiated at this point in the exchange and your punch would overdo it. Necessity is fundamental to the T&P rule.

Impact: In conjunction with Necessity is Impact, which can mostly be assessed by the question, "Will my humor add value, or make me look really stupid?" Try to exercise the power of forethought and project how your comic nugget will be received by your audience. This could certainly range from laughter so robust that neighboring businesses call the police, to a silence so uncomfortable that a gurgling stomach is a welcome symphony.

Consequence: If you cannot reasonably project the possible consequence of your workplace mirth, then simply don't do it. In other words, if you are just launching humor out there without assessing possible consequences (good or bad) then it is unequivocally NOT the time nor place.

Some possible consequences that can and do occur:

Good consequences: respect, appreciation, needed laughs, tension diffused, good sentiments, job security, employee productivity, unity, positive work environment, strong self-esteem, teamwork, promotions, raises, employee loyalty and engagement, camaraderie,...All very desirable outcomes that can and do happen when adherence to Time and Place happens.

Bad consequences: retribution, loss of respect, demotion, offended parties, harassment charges, lawsuits, low morale, lack of productivity, violence, misunderstandings, disciplinary action, probation, garnished wages, death threats, criminal charges, slashed tires, smashed windshield, bludgeoning, bodily harm, protests, strikes, terrorism, Middle East warfare, leprosy, you get the idea.

Remember the criterion is two-fold: Time *and* Place. You need to nail down both before making merry. Here are two examples where only half of the rule is right.

Right Time/Wrong Place: *Jason brings a werewolf mask to work on Halloween. He wears it into a managers' meeting where he growls at people and bays at the fluorescent "moon." All in good fun.*

Not necessarily funny, but the timing's right. The nature of the meeting does not call for this level of physical levity, however. Not to mention the fact that Janet is in attendance. Janet's daughter was eaten by wolves a few weeks earlier.

On the good side, Jason has picked the right *time* to loosen up and help others do the same: Halloween, or any other holiday season. Not all companies allow masks or other costumes but Jason's company obviously does, and in the spirit of mirth management, Jason joins in. It is, overall, the right time. The business meeting, particularly one with a woman whose offspring was recently consumed by White Fang, was not the right *place*.

Wrong Time/Right Place: *Once outside the meeting (wrong place) Jason hustles over to a group of his employees sullenly grouped around the break room ping-pong table. Two employees half-heartedly hit the ball back and forth. Jason puts the mask back on and starts the werewolf routine. When one of the player's shots lands off the table Jason howls, "Ow ow owwwwwwwuuuut of bow bow bowwwwwwu uuuunnndddssss.!"*

Again, this is just goofing around. It's levity, pure and simple. It's not necessarily funny to most, but it's light. The group of a half dozen shakes their heads and some walk off. Their reaction is decidedly cold.

And why wouldn't it be? While the break room is the perfect *place* for Jason's inanity, his announcement one hour earlier that there would be no holiday bonuses and that exactly half of his employees could expect to be fired by day's end cast a slight pall over the festivities. Not a good *time* to play the foo-foo-fooooooooooool.

To recap, the Time and Place Rule can be understood as follows:

Before workplace humor is publicly launched, careful consideration of its propriety can be satisfied by an affirmative response to one question, namely: Does this humor fit the occasion? By considering Necessity, Impact, and Consequence the answer should be clear.

In short, the Time and Place rule helps determine if your attempts to lighten things up safely count as…

Appropriate Workplace Humor

By now you understand the need for discretion in your attempts at creating a mood of mirth at work. If you adhere to the fundamental principles of Time and Place the resulting effects should be totally appropriate. On the other hand, judgment and discretion are critical to the T&P rule working, and some of us possess about as much good judgment as a juror in the Simpson trial.

So, the purpose of the next few pages is to illustrate some more practical examples and ideas of workplace merriment that fit the T&P criteria, and some areas you'll likely want to avoid. For example, check out the following admittedly extreme scenario:

Mr. Festerton: Hey, Claire, come here for a second, I've got something I need to show you.

Claire: Yes, sir, what is it?

Mr. Festerton: I bought something for my wife for our anniversary and I'm worried it may not fit. You're about her size. Would you mind trying it on? Or at least holding it up to you?

Claire: What is it?

Mr. Festerton hands her a silicone breast implant bag and laughs.

Claire blanches.

Mr. Festerton: Just kidding. Come on.

Funny? Maybe to a select few. That's the kind of humor that is best enjoyed among high school sophomore boys. Appropriate? Not only is it totally inappropriate and unfunny among socializing adults, but can also be considered sexual harassment and grounds for legal action. Watch out. Clearly, Festerton has no use for T&P since he doesn't appear to possess a discretionary bone in his body. Festerton couldn't pour judgment from a boot if the instructions were written on the heel.

Any bit of levity that requires the disclaimer, "Just kidding" should categorically be exorcised from your arsenal. Too often, this type of humor winds up hurting feelings or exposing true hostility. Sadly, most offenders using the "just kidding" excuse are lying. They are, in fact, saying what they truly feel or think, and nearly every time the target of their "joke" takes it as an authentic insult. To *kid* means to "mock playfully" or "to engage in good-humored fooling," but in the office it is rarely interpreted as being so innocent. It's best to simply not to do it.

LEADING WITH LEVITY THROUGHOUT HISTORY

In 1945, though Winston Churchill was instrumental in winning WWII, he lost his re-election bid for Prime Minister. When the news came out, Churchill was taking a bath.

He remarked, "They have a perfect right to kick me out. That is democracy."

When he was offered the Order of the Garter, he asked "Why should I accept the Order of the Garter, when the British people have just given me the Order of the Boot?"

For all that he had accomplished he had every reason to be bitter. Fortunately he kept his sense of humor even in trying circumstances, and was back at the reins in 1951.

Churchhill's humor

- In 1943, Churchill remarked: "I always avoid prophesying beforehand, because it is much better policy to prophesy after the event has already taken place."

- Once, when handed a lengthy memorandum, Churchill remarked "This paper by its very length defends itself against the risk of being read."

Dr. Joni Johnston has this to say, "Apparently, not all humor is created equal. Research has shown that there is a distinctive difference in the health benefits of positive and negative humor. Negative humor, i.e., humor that is exclusive or offensive, does not have the same positive physiological effects on one's body and mind. Apparently, our bodies are as sensitive as our feelings; we physiologically respond to hurtful remarks as if our bodies were under attack. Which, in some ways, is true."

By the same token, and in the spirit of lightening up, we all need to go a little easier on people who make comic blunders and mirth mistakes. If you truly lead with levity, you're far more likely to blow off somebody's offensive remark or caustic verbiage. Nobody's perfect and it's not life or death. If somebody says something a little edgy or offensive, react appropriately and move on. Jesus of Nazareth, 2000 years ago, taught that people should be longsuffering and not easily offended. That's pretty solid advice from one of history's great leaders.

Levity means *lightness* after all, as in "lighten up." Too often, well-meaning and innocent bits of mirth that didn't quite hit the mark are taken far too seriously. I was recently speaking to an unexpectedly small group of leaders at a Texas construction company. Fully a half-hour into the presentation a woman came into the meeting and took a seat. As small as the room was it would have been ridiculous *not* to acknowledge her presence, and her rather conspicuous tardiness.

I said something like, "Well, you're a half hour late, but thanks for coming; you've doubled our attendance. So we appreciate it." The four or five others laughed, enjoying the little jab aimed at our low attendance. She sneered at me.

After the session, she came straight to me and let me have it. "You know the little comment about me being late was out of line," she chided. "It was totally inappropriate and unprofessional."

"That's funny," I said. "I thought your waltzing into my presentation a half hour late was equally unprofessional."

"How dare you—I'm the client!" she spat.

"How dare *you?*" I replied. "I'm the guest speaker!"

Needless to say, she spun on her proverbial heels and huffed out of the room. One of her coworkers was overheard saying, "Boy, she really needs to *lighten up.*"

Amen, brother. But I digress.

In general, strive for humor that is inclusive, creative and captures our human essence. All of us know that sexist, racist, ageist jokes and crude humor are not only inappropriate, but can lead to sanctions, termination or even lawsuits. In addition, be sensitive when telling jokes involving terminations, RIFs and personal tragedies. Their hurt can linger long after the fact.

Most people have no desire to offend anyone. The number one reason humor backfires at work is when a manager or employee makes the dangerous assumption that everyone is like s/he is. It's easy to assume that everyone has our sense of humor, to believe that a person will react the way we would, to think that anyone who looks like us has same values and beliefs. Here are the five most common forms of this assumption – and why they don't work.

She Has No Sense Of Humor . . .

I've been around the block a time or two and I've never met anyone with no sense of humor. I have, alas, met people who didn't have *my* sense of humor. While laughter is universal, humor is not; it varies from person to person.

I Hope This Doesn't Offend Anyone . . .

Few of us would think prefacing a punch with "I hope this doesn't hurt" gives us permission to slug someone, but often we think a warning to our colleagues that we are about to tell a risqué joke alleviates us from its impact. While this preface might have good intentions, it doesn't let us off the hook in a work environment. Much better to err on the side of caution and, if you think it might offend someone, save it for the Friday night bowling league.

But I Thought We Were The Same . . .

I was once in a meeting where the leader looked around the room, noticed there were no individuals of Asian descent present, and proceeded to tell a very racist joke. What he didn't realize is that his customer – also in the room – was the proud mother of a darling Chinese girl. Needless to say, this humorous attempt backfired and the manager had to eat serious crow to repair the relationship.

But We Were At Lunch . . .

Just because we've left the building doesn't mean we've left our work roles behind. Managers, in particular, may fall prey to the temptation to show their employees that, outside of work, they can party hardy with the best of them. The problem is that their employees often don't understand the same distinction between work and play and may see a manager's rowdy humor at happy hour as "permission" to repeat it in the office first thing Monday morning.

Here are a few general guidelines to ensure appropriate workplace humor provided by a specialized staffing agency, The Creative Group:

Say No To Sarcasm

People often use humor as an indirect way of berating others. Here's an example: "I can't believe you're here on time--what's the occasion?" Sarcasm is rarely a good idea. If a comment is negative and rings somewhat true, don't say it. I know from personal experience how difficult this one can be to perfect.

Break The Chain

Think twice before you email a joke to a long list of coworkers. This may annoy rather than amuse, and it may be against company policy. Try to tailor your humor to the individual. A personal touch will make a more memorable impression.

Under-do It

Making a funny comment to diffuse tension during a meeting is a great idea, but don't turn it into a stand-up routine followed by five more jokes. You don't want to look like you're trying too hard. Effortless mastery--or at least the appearance of ease--is the key to good comedy.

Laugh With Others

You can be perceived as having a great sense of humor without ever telling a joke. Just tune in to the humor styles of those around you and share in their laughter. Again, humor is give and take. You can certainly afford to take more than you give…especially if those you're giving to ask for the receipt.

CHAPTER 6

Crows Feet and Rosy Cheeks

A merry heart maketh a cheerful countenance.
King Solomon

At its foundation, management by mirth is a question of character. What kind do you have? Do you feel a sense of ease and levity right now? Are you reading this book with a furrowed brow and a skeptical sneer? If so, this chapter is dying for you to read it. Chapters have feelings too, you know.

Some people seem to exude a natural sense of happiness. Let's be random. Take Julie Andrews, for example. You probably didn't expect that one. The image of her that just popped into your head when I said, "Take Julie Andrews, for example" is probably one of her from 'The Sound of Music' or 'Mary Poppins.' Does she look ticked off or frustrated in your head? Are her nostrils heaving like a winded racehorse?

If your image of her is anything like mine, she is grinning or flat-out smiling. Her eyes are bright and shining. You simply cannot imagine or even remember a time when Julie Andrews looked as though she gave two spoonfuls of sugar about Liesel "going on 17" or the German army setting up camp in their mud room. This is a frau that's got the twinkly-eye thing going on, and keeps a carefree perspective.

Couple her *sense* of humor with her ability to be funny and that's a great leader. You remember how she took all those kids and got them singing "Doe a Deer" wearing matching jumpsuits like a bunch of little pansies? That's not easy, especially with the older boys. I think Free-drick was already questioning who he was, when along comes this grinning Pied Piper cleverly convincing him to don froofy culottes and sing falsetto rounds. She was good.

But, of course that's just a character Andrews played. Can a person really be expected to be that chipper all the time in real life? It's doubtful and unrealistic. Still, Andrews breathed the life into the Maria character and undoubtedly was cast for the role partly because of the friendly, optimistic quality she emits in her everyday persona. Ok, now the real test: Would Fraulein Maria make a good organizational leader? You bet your sweet lederhosen.

The best of leaders have that smile in their eyes. It is pervasive in all they do, in all their conversations and actions. When you smile and laugh your eyes crinkle a little and your cheeks color. You send out a positive, easy-going vibe. You become a little like Santa Claus. And who wouldn't do just about anything for 'Jolly Ole,' if he asked? Stephen R. Covey describes it this way:

"Their countenances...are cheerful, pleasant, happy. Their attitude is optimistic, positive, upbeat. Their spirit is enthusiastic, hopeful, believing.

This positive energy is like an energy field or an aura that surrounds them and that similarly charges or changes weaker, negative energy fields around them. They also attract and magnify smaller positive energy fields. When they come into contact with strong, negative energy sources, they tend either to neutralize or to sidestep this negative energy. Sometimes they will simply leave it, walking away from its poisonous orbit. Wisdom gives them a sense of how strong it is and a sense of humor and of timing in dealing with it."

Those around you naturally feel a little better. Management consultant Fred Pryor points out that an element of fun at work has several benefits including the fact that "happy employees tend to be healthy employees and, therefore, are on the job instead of at home taking sick leave." With more energy, vigor and yes, vim (great word, vim) your people are far more likely to produce at higher and more sustainable levels.

Do you remember *Who Framed Roger Rabbit?* Whenever Eddie (Bob Hoskins) went to Toon Town the Toons were singing an old song from the 30s called *Smile, Darn Ya, Smile.* Annoying little number, really. But it sure sticks in my head, especially when I feel an attack of JawClench or BrowKnit coming on.

Smile, Darn Ya', Smile

Words by Chas. O'Flynn and Jack Meskill, Music by Max Rich - 1931

Verse:
Let's all get to -geth -er with this one thought in mind,
Make this world a bet -ter, bright -er place.
Tell each "Blue Nose" and "Joy Kill -er" you ev -er find
"Hey there! Wipe that frown right off your face."

Chorus:
Smile, Darn Ya', Smile,
You know this old world is a great world af -ter all.
Smile, Darn Ya', Smile,
And right a -way watch "La -dy Luck" pay you a call.
Things are nev -er black as they are paint -ed,
Time for you and joy to get ac -quaint -ed.
Make life worth while
Come on and
Smile, Darn Ya', Smile.

"Time for you and joy to get acquainted." When was the last time you smiled enough to feel joy?

It may be just dumb to presume that you smile when you arise each day, excited to get to work. But if you do, you know the almost immediate positive effect this very elementary act can have. If you don't, if you're not smiling at yourself in the mirror each morning, try it. And I mean really smile, think of something that's positive and good and let it force a grin. You'll quickly find your mood change. Unless of course your smile could stop a charging pit bull and you absolutely hate it, then please—for the love—don't look at your smile in the mirror. Lose the reflection and just smile. We don't want this to turn into a self-esteem problem involving an argument with your father from 1973 and you winding up suicidal.

Do you know people who seem to be grinning all the time? You know the ones that have that look like they just opened a Christmas present. We typically conclude that a person that wears a perma-smile is either hiding something or needs professional help.

But, maybe these bright and beaming mutants are just born that way. Certainly there must be those who are genetically predisposed to a pleasant nature. And though I suppose that to be the case, I'm more inclined to believe that happy people make themselves happy. They simply choose to be happy and manifest it outwardly, and by so doing display a remarkable control over external influences.

Happy and smiling people tend to brighten everything and everyone around them. Most of us are drawn to them. We want to soak up some of that positive energy and humor. Imagine working for someone like that. Does it sound like the kind of work environment where you might be more productive and satisfied? If your boss can get you to temporarily forget about your concerns at home and other stresses of life, you'll be able to focus more energy on work. Makes sense. Again, it seems overly simple. In principle, it is. But practically speaking we aren't exactly suffering from a glut of cheerful and jovial managers.

Author Harvey Hornstein (real name!), Ph.D., estimates that 90 percent of the U.S. work force has been subjected to abusive behavior at some time. He bases his conclusions on a survey of nearly 1,000 workers over eight years. Who needs abusive behavior at work? Can't we get enough of that at home? Jeffrey Gitomer (The Sales Bible) says that a grumpy boss equals low morale, which equals high staff turnover.

You may never have told a joke or shared a laugh with a coworker. And maybe you never will. Fine. That's up to you. We're not in business for entertainment's sake. Just kill the grumpy stuff. Lighten up. Allow others to enjoy levity; it goes a long way.

Where's the smile in your eyes? In your voice? Radio broadcasters and voiceover professionals—especially those in advertising—know that having a "smile in your voice" brings a fresh, energetic read to even the most mundane traffic reports or grocery store commercials. That can certainly apply to telephone conversations. It's easy to sound like a monotone drone over the phone. If we're in a sour mood or feeling exhausted—without the face-to-face pressure of being "on"—our telephone voice can send very confusing or even negative signals.

And though the telephone is the most common breeding ground for cheerless vocal exchanges, you've got to be on your toes at all times.

> *The countenance is the portrait of the soul,*
> *and the eyes mark its intentions.*
> *Marcus Tullius Cicero*

But, back to the eyes. Do yours sparkle, shine, radiate, glimmer, twinkle, even dance? Typical BKs and JCs have a flame of stress, concern, anger, exhaustion, or fear constantly alit in their eyes, not unlike the blue pilot light on your furnace. When their conflict or issue thermostat requires it, the pilot flares to life and blasts gusts of hot air through their various vents and registers. (All right, enough with the heater analogy.) Think about it; if the eyes are the windows of the soul, do your employees rightly assume that your soul is drenched in pure evil after spending 30 seconds talking face to face with you?

Check out your "crow's feet" if you've got them. How deep are they? How much effort does it take to get them to appear? Age will have a little to do with it, but here's the real question: How'd you acquire them? From a lifetime of BrowKnitting and scowling/squinting, or are they the result of decades of smiling and laughing? It's never too late to make the transition. After all, your wrinkles and folds continue to form and deepen through the years. Commit now to increasing your "laugh lines" and go a little easier on your forehead and brow. Un-knit your brow and loosen your jaw, your Clint Eastwood perturbed look will start to fade.

A children's song goes like this:

> *If you chance to meet a frown*
> *Do not let it stay*
> *Quickly turn it upside down*
> *And smile that frown away!*
>
> *No one likes a frowny face*
> *Change it for a smile*
> *Make the world a better place*
> *By smiling all the while*

When your employees begin to sense a smile in your countenance—even when you're not actually smiling—they will start to feel more at ease around you. They will naturally like you better, and if they actually like you, well you know the rest.

Happy boss: happy worker: happy customer: happy shareholder: happy boss: happy worker (repeat).

All this sounds lovely, but what if you're just *not happy*? Life is so much more than work. Maybe you've had some major (or minor) personal setbacks. Your spouse kicked you out. Your children are getting into trouble. Your father was recently spotted wearing women's bedroom attire.

Whatever the case, most people—including you—suffer hardships and trials outside of work almost incessantly, not to mention the pressure and stress at work. Wearing a smile and happy demeanor to the office presupposes that you were happy before you got to work, that you're not just putting on a show for the troop's morale. But even if you are, is that so bad? When you recognize the universality of "hard times on the homefront" it helps you "*put on* a happy face" to not only cheer yourself up, but to establish an environment where your people can distance themselves from their own non-work burdens.

It's almost inconceivable that a leader could show up to work every single day with a bright countenance, put-on or authentic. But if you set it as a goal, you'll succeed in infusing much-needed levity into your workplace, thus, when going through your own rough times your now loyal and happy employees can be there for *you*.

CHAPTER 7

Good For What Ails You

A merry heart doeth good like a medicine.
Proverbs 17:22

Is your workplace ill? Do you sense the sickness permeating through the cubicles like a plague? It's not a seasonal bug or virus. It isn't the dreaded 24-hour flu or a hacking cough that doesn't produce. Where laughter and humor have vanished, in their place you'll find a team or department that doesn't produce. Why? Their spirits are ailing. They need a little levity.

It seems that those with a sense of humor are better communicators and better team players. Studies have shown that happy workers are more productive. In fact, a researcher at California State University found that humor could help the employees to release tension. Consequently, they can concentrate on their work more efficiently. What's more, employees who enjoy interacting with their co-workers aren't as likely to be distracted, or absent from work.

Think about it. First, your people show up for work. That's good. But once there, they feel higher levels of satisfaction and yes, glee, which in turn ratchets up their focus and productivity. All because you've caught the vision of frequent and meaningful Time&Place

levity. The lighter the mood, the easier it is to free up the mind. Unleash creativity. Make discoveries. Contribute with impact.

Research conducted by psychologist Dr. Ashton Trice at Mary Baldwin College in Virginia showed that humor helps us think. When people feel stuck on important projects, they tend to feel angry or depressed. This negative mood can interfere with subsequent performance. According to Dr. Trice's research, taking time out to laugh can help us to get rid of negative feelings and allow us to return to a task or move on to another project unaffected by past defeat.

Laughter is good for the soul and body.

How else do you think George Burns lasted as long as he did smoking all those cigars? What was he when he died—111? Bob Hope kept it light well into his 90s. Gordon B. Hinckley, president of the Church of Jesus Christ of Latter-day Saints is 95 and still very active, lucid, spunky, and most significantly, uses humor and levity in his lectures and teachings.

> *We need to have a little humor in our lives. We better take seriously that which should be taken seriously, but at the same time we can bring in a touch of humor now and again. If the time ever comes when we can't smile at ourselves, it will be a sad time.*
> *– Gordon B. Hinckley*

Hinckley has long been known as a charismatic and powerful leader and his trademark humor is one of the qualities that endear him to millions of faithful followers. During a very hot afternoon session of the church's general conference in the famed Mormon Tabernacle the air conditioning was on the blink. Hinckley stood up and addressed the sweaty congregation, "It's warm. We're sorry. But it's not as warm as it's going to get if you don't repent!"

There is a link between sense of humor and longevity, Dr. Raymond J. Moody reports, and there is also a definite anesthetic effect of laughter, an 'inverse relationship between humor and pain.' There is also some evidence, though not conclusive, that laughter triggers the brain to release catecholamine hormones, which in turn cause the release of endorphins, the body's natural painkiller.

"We believe laughing is good for your health," said Michael Miller of the University of Maryland School of Medicine in Baltimore. "And we think we have evidence to show why that's the case."

In a 2000 study, Miller and some colleagues examined the connection between blood vessels' ability to expand (vasodilatation) and laughter. They found that when vasodilatation is poor, it can increase one's risk of heart attack and stroke.

The study took 20 adults who watched clips of a violent movie (probably "Fried Green Tomatoes") and a humorous movie and then had their vasodilatation tested. They found that blood flow was significantly reduced by about 35 percent in 14 of the 20 volunteers who saw the stressful film, a resounding endorsement to steer clear of anything starring Shirley Maclaine.

Does this resonate with you? Stress reduces blood flow. Let me type that slowly so you don't read it too quickly: Stress reduces blood flow. And you know all that flowing blood? Yeah, that keeps your heart beating and your brain alive.

On the other hand, blood flow increased by 22 percent in 19 of the 20 volunteers after watching the funny movie. The 20th person undoubtedly was a full on Brow-Knitting Jaw Clencher who dug his or her nails into the chair arms like a tortured prisoner.

And get this! Miller and his research team said the improvement in blood flow experienced by most all participants after laughter was equal to the improvements seen after a 15- to 30-minute workout!

Now, don't get any funny ideas that you can chuck your resolve to lose 20 pounds through diet and exercise by simply laughing more. While heavy bouts of laughter temporarily burn a few more calories and increase blood flow, it won't produce a Brad Pitt physique.

However, combining exercise with humor could result in the murder of a pair of avian with a single rock-like projectile. Imagine 30 minutes on a treadmill while watching your favorite comedy. Do you have a gym at work? Download an old Eddie Murphy, Cheech and Chong, or Steve Martin concert album onto your Ipod and bust a gut while you bust your butt.

Lee Berk, an associate professor of health promotion and education at Loma Linda University in California said, "Laughter is not dissimilar from exercise. It's not going to cure someone from stage three cancer, but in terms of prevention it does make sense. In a sense, we have our own apothecary on our shoulders. Positive emotions such as laughter affect your biology."

Miller and his team conducted another study that involved 300 people. He found that persons who already had heart disease "responded less humorously to everyday life situations." Not only did these people laugh less, even when the situation was positive, but they also showed more signs of anger and hostility.

The obvious reaction here is: Duh. How much money did they spend to determine that people with heart disease aren't finding a lot to laugh about? The real question I'd like to know is, were these people always angry and hostile? Did they find humor in everyday life before they were diagnosed? Because if not then maybe you could make a real tenuous link between being a grump and getting heart disease. That conclusion coupled with the vasodilatation study could make a pretty good case to "lighten up or die." Research like this will never be able to prove causation but the inference is clear: Laughter is good for you.

Whether you have heart disease or not, you have to admit that it would be nice to eliminate any anger or hostility you may experience personally or in your work environment. It may be as simple as finding a quiet place to laugh on your own or share a funny story with one of your co-workers.

You know how Weight Watchers and other diets have you count your daily calories to better your health and fitness; by the same token you can up your daily laugh count with a goal. According to Barbara Bartlein, R.N., M.S.W., "Children laugh approximately 80 to 100 times per day (other sources call this figure low). By the time we reach adulthood, we laugh only 5-6 times per day. You only need to watch children to appreciate the relationship between humor and enjoying life. Children will laugh at anything! If you ask them, "What's so funny?" they may say something like, "He looked at me!"

But how does it actually work? How is it that my body can benefit from a simple laugh? Well, it's actually not that simple physiologically. It's beautifully complicated. "Humor and, its partner, laughter," says Steven M. Sultanoff, Ph.D. "activate the physiological systems including the muscular, respiratory, cardiovascular, and skeletal. In fact, we may even lose muscle control, as many of us have, when we laugh so hard that we fall down or wet our pants."

(The staining of one's drawers is by far the acme of comic measurement; it may not necessarily boost higher levels of workplace loyalty and success, but it will most certainly become a legendary story to tell for those who witnessed it.)

"Laughter has been labeled a jogging and juggling of the internal organs. When we laugh we feel physically better, and after laughter we feel lighter and more relaxed."

Again, remember the times you've lost control of your body and fallen to the ground in an aching heap of laughs. That level of laughter produces a natural high that is sweet to the senses. If you've never had such a moment, you've missed one of the greatest experiences an individual could ever have (minus the soaked undies, of course).

Physiologically, laughter enhances the immune system, starts the brain's natural painkillers flowing and reduces stress, a major contributor to a variety of physical problems, according to Ann Weeks, a Louisville-based therapist and former president of the Association for Therapeutic humor. The proper use of humor and laughter in the workplace means less sick days. So, if you're taking a sick day because you are actually sick (for once) by all means pop in "Raising Arizona" instead of "Raisin in the Sun." Laugh yourself to a quicker recovery.

From **The Biology of Humor**, by W.F. Fry, "Vigorous laughter is stimulating, increasing heart rate, blood pressure, and circulation; circulating immune substance effectiveness, pulmonary ventilation, and alertness; and exercising the skeletal muscles. Following laughter there is a brief period during which blood pressure drops and heart rate, respiratory rate, and muscle activity decrease, resulting in relaxation."

Sounds a little like sex, doesn't it?

Feels like a good time to move away from the body and talk a little about how levity benefits the soul.

Then come jesters, musicians and trained dwarfs,
And singing girls from the land of Ti-ti,
To delight the ear and eye
And bring mirth to the mind.
—Sima Xiangru (ca. 179-117 B.C.), *Rhapsody on the Shanglin Park*

Centuries ago in China, England, Turkey or Chicken Salad, the court jester was often summoned to try to lift the monarch out of an angry or melancholic mood. Certainly, there was no shortage of stress in the life of royalty in medieval times (imagine the constant threat of an assassin's arrow from a grassy knoll whilst waving to villagers from an open-roofed carriage), and they understood the magic of mirth in settling their psyches.

Jeanne Segal, Ph.D., Managing Editor of Helpguide.org provides a wonderful list of how humor can boost our mental health:

- *Humor enhances our ability to affiliate or connect with others.* By acting as a social lubricant, humor gets us all greasy and slimy…and helps us loosen up. It's a lot easier to connect with others when you feel this way.

- *Humor helps us replace distressing emotions with pleasurable feelings.* You cannot feel angry, depressed, anxious, guilty, or resentful and experience humor at the same time.

- *Lacking humor will cause one's thought processes to stagnate leading to increased distress.* The more you allow humor to rattle around your head, the more freed up your thoughts become. JawClenching restricts your ability to generate good ideas. Lighten up.

- *Humor changes behavior.* When we experience humor we talk more, make more eye contact with others, touch others, etc.

- *Humor increases energy.* With increased energy we may perform activities that we might otherwise avoid, and get more done in shorter order.

- *Humor is good for mental health because it makes us feel good!*

Easier said than done? Dr. Segal continues with some specific ways in which to use laughter to improve our mood and overall enjoyment of life:

Attempt to laugh at situations rather than bemoan them – this helps improve our disposition and the disposition of those around us.

I'm guessing that you've been around someone who has nothing positive to say about anything. "I hate Mondays." "This job sucks."

"I've been probed by aliens." Do you like to be around that person? Does anyone? Are you that person? To quote Monty Python's *Life of Brian*, "Always look on the bright side of life." Laugh. Smile. Giggle. No matter how stressful work may be, nobody's going to die for it. Even military leaders, as evidenced in previous chapters, know humor works and their people actually *could* die.

Use cathartic laughter to release pent-up feelings of anger and frustration in socially acceptable ways.

In some cases, the court jester's job was to diffuse tense situations, even battles, by acting the fool. The combatants would get caught up in laughter and become distracted. The harder they cackled, the more they released angry emotions harmlessly. While sharing a good laugh together the lust for fighting would wane. Both parties would agree to disagree and be done with it. (Eventually they would disembowel one another, but what are you going to do?)

> We must laugh at man to avoid crying for him.
> Napoleon Bonaparte

Lower anxiety by visualizing a humorous situation to replace the view of an anxiety-producing situation.

We've all heard the one about visualizing your audience in their underwear if you're nervous about giving a public speech. Believe it or not, this technique works. Sometimes I'm so relaxed before giving a speech that I'll do it in my underwear just to have some anxiety. Whatever gives you mental anxiety, meet it head on in your mind and then think about it a little left of center.

Considering the cumulative emotional and physical benefits of humor it may be tempting to think, "Wow. All I have to do is laugh a little more and voila! No depression, no cancer and I'll forever be at my ideal body weight."

But remember that there is no research that proves that humor heals any illness. The best we can do is infer that humor has curative effects. The Association for Applied and Therapeutic Humor says it best: "An inference that humor is healing can be drawn, for example, in the following way: A wealth of research has indicated that distressing emotions (depression, anger, anxiety, and stress) are all related to heart disease. Humor directly changes distressing emotions. Therefore Humor may reduce the risk of heart disease." *(What Is Humor?, Steven M. Sultanoff, PhD).* Dr. Sultanoff further says that there is no research indicating that endorphins are secreted during laughter, a commonly held belief. However, saying out loud something like, "You're such an endorphin" will probably get you chuckling.

CHAPTER 8

Self-Deprecating Humor

In 1958, then-Senator John F. Kennedy was already leading the pack for the Democratic presidential nomination, but many in Washington still dismissed him as the brash son of a wealthy and unscrupulous man, a father too eager to bankroll his son's upcoming bid for the White House. Speaking at the Capitol Hilton before an audience of such skeptics, Kennedy held up what he said was a telegram from his "generous daddy" and read it aloud: "Jack, Don't spend one dime more than is necessary. I'll be damned if I am going to pay for a landslide."

The art of self-deprecating humor does not come easily to most. It requires a healthy sense of self-esteem and a keen understanding of its target audience. It is not a quality that many leaders possess. Author Mark Katz put it this way, "Self-deprecating humor comes naturally to only the most skillful practitioners of public power and your average Jew."

In the typical workplace opinions, attitudes, and scuttle are bounced around like a beach ball. Inevitably the subject of this gossip will include management, i.e., you. And while much of the chattel is completely ungrounded in truth whatsoever, still you must keep your finger on its pulse. Because chances are good that you'll discover at the heart of it are some bits of public opinion that you can use. When you become aware of others' feelings of you as a leader—or as a person—it provides you with a valuable 2nd and 3rd party perspective of yourself.

If you keep your ear to the ground or rely on the word of a loyal employee you'll be up to date on your "approval ratings." Who wouldn't want a barometer of how one is doing as a leader? And who better to evaluate you than those whom you lead? Candid and untainted feedback from an "insider" or from simply fine-tuning your own ear will arm you with information needed to improve you as a leader.

When you are accurately apprised of how people feel about you and what they think and say about you, you're ready to dive into the high-return world of self-effacement.

But first it bears asking, "To what end?" Why should you care about developing and honing the art of comedic humility? Dr. Terry L. Paulson describes self-depreciating humor this way. "When you tell a story that pokes fun at yourself gently, it acts as a social lubricant that says, 'Hey, this person is a human being, someone at ease with life, and we can feel the same way'."

Business author Terry Maher adds, "Self-deprecating humor is a great way for executives and managers to put themselves on the same level as their subordinates. It shows they can take a joke, that they too put their pants or their pantyhose on one leg at a time."

LEADING WITH LEVITY THROUGHOUT HISTORY

Her Majesty Queen Elizabeth The Queen Mother was an avid sportswoman. She loved to fish and was an enthusiastic horseracing fan. She was also reputed to have had a keen sense of humor. In reference to the large numbers of homosexuals on the royal staff, the Queen Mother reputed once to have called to the kitchen, "When you old queens are done gossiping, this old queen would like a drink."

A new manager was obligated to post a lengthy list of rules right after being promoted to the position, hardly the best rapport builder. He posted the list all right, but he signed it at the bottom, "A. Hitler, Gruppenfuehrer." His superior snatched it off the wall, calling it "inappropriate." Perhaps. But by then everyone had already seen it.

"We'd read the rules," one worker reports. "We figured the *Gruppenfuehrer* was going to enforce them. We knew the iron fist was there, and we appreciated that he'd stuck it in a velvet glove and used it to poke a little fun at himself. Otherwise we'd have seen it as a new guy coming in and throwing his weight around."

Another mid-level manager had a grumpy looking doll with a tape recorder inside that he'd programmed to say, "Get your mangy butts back on the job and stop wasting the company's time." The doll would deliver the message whenever the manager decided it was needed. People took the hint, and nobody was offended.

As humor expert Malcolm Kushner says, "Learn to take your work seriously without taking yourself so seriously. No matter how serious your work or topic, it's always safe to poke fun at yourself."

It's a safe bet that someone like Rodney Dangerfield comes to mind when discussing self-effacement. In fact, generally speaking, workplace humor—giving or receiving—is associated with men. But Gina Berreca in Ms. Magazine pointed out that self-deprecating humor is acceptable as feminine. That making fun of yourself — or, by extension, other women — is okay comes across clearly to young women. Penny Marshall claims that she would "make fun of myself before anybody else could. I had braces and my hair in a ponytail — real attractive…So I would always hit before anyone could hit me. Self-defacing humor is my forte."

The very word choice of "self-defacing" is interesting here, since by using a comic mask, Marshall seems to have found a way early in life to put on a new face. Many funny women found out in childhood or early adolescence that self-deprecating humor can draw fire. Phyllis

Diller said that becoming funny was her way of "adjusting to puberty. When I reached that self-conscious age where I looked like Olive Oyl and wanted to look like Jean Harlow, I knew something had to be done. From 12 on, the only way to handle the terror of social situations was comedy — break the ice, make everybody laugh. I did it to make people feel more relaxed, including myself."

Berreca says women grow up learning that they can defuse a situation by turning themselves into self-effacing diversions, taking a little bit out of themselves in order to make others happy.

But, again, it's important to really know how people feel before you start auto-shredding. Let's say you take a crack at self-effacing humor. You say to your team over lunch—on you—in a fine restaurant, "I know everybody thinks I'm a cheapskate, but that's only because I'm fanatically obsessive about never spending one red cent more than would absolutely be necessary." Nice bit of humor, but the truth is nobody thinks you're cheap. That's not their perception of you; actually they think you're incompetent. And by using self-deprecation to address an imagined issue, you've just solidified their belief that you are, in fact, an idiot. Though buying them a fancy lunch won't hurt your rep.

Naturally, it's easier for public leaders to become privy to how those they govern perceive them; they have the press. When Dan Quayle was Vice President he made several public gaffes. We all remember his misspelling of the word 'potato' and the subsequent argument with a small schoolboy. Quayle was mercilessly raked over the coals throughout Bush's entire administration. A few small and simple mistakes became the unending subject of late-night monologues, comedy sketches and talk show rants.

Dan Quayle was and is a good man and a fine leader. He was elected to US Congress at 29. Then, four years later, elected to the Senate. After a couple of successful terms as Senator Quayle he was selected as running mate to eventual President George Bush. He was boy-wonder in D.C. for most of the late 70s and 80s. Then in his highest-profile position, as VP, he made a few "ignorant" comments (probably no more than he or anyone is prone to make) and was vilified for the rest of his political career.

Taking his lickings in stride and understanding the futility of battling with the media-fueled public perception of his persona, Quayle chose the high road of embracing his image. Here's just one bit of self-effacement from Quayle as reported in the LA Times, May 1989:

"The other day [President Bush, the dad] said, 'I know you've had some rough times, and I want to do something that will show the nation what faith I have in you, in your maturity and sense of responsibility. (He paused, then said) Would you like a puppy?'"

In another nod to the prevailing sentiment of mockery, Quayle said to a group in Eau Claire, Wisconsin, "I've been told to keep my remarks relatively brief. I understand Quayle-hunting season begins at noon."

Even before his marital problems and personal indiscretions became the fodder of legendary character disembowelment, President Bill Clinton had to use self-deprecation to survive. Author Mark Katz wrote a book—*Clinton and Me*—about his experiences as a writer with the president.

"As the designated White House in-house humorist, it was my job to guide him through Washington's odd humor rituals with my best and funniest suggestions for the things he might say. Somewhere in the course of my career that bridged the world of humor and politics, I had absorbed the first rule of successful presidential mirth-making. From Teddy Roosevelt ("Speak softly and carry a big stick.") to Ronald Reagan ("I am not worried about the deficit. It is big enough to take care of itself."), the most popular presidents have used wit to steal the ammunition from their critics as the best way to defend themselves.

"Bill Clinton is as smart as any person who's held the office, perfectly capable of generating witticism and winning over a crowd. But when being tortured endlessly by Beltway critics, even he needed a little help. Clinton had become accustomed to using humor as a barbed weapon; I tried to coax out of him something new--not Kennedy's entirely self-deprecating voice, nor his old, slightly venomous brand of humor, but a new style of self-effacing wit with a bit of a bite. In the end, Clinton did it his way: self-deprecating jibes, but with an elbow to his attackers, too."

In 1993, Clinton's presidency had gotten off to a rocky start and, using Katz's material at one of his first big Washington dinners, declared: "I don't think I'm doing that badly. After his First Hundred Days in office, William Henry Harrison had already been dead for 68 days!"

The power of self-deprecating humor to defuse an otherwise tense or difficult situation is beyond dispute. In Washington politics, it's a given. George W. Bush has skillfully used humor, both before and after he became president. Washington, D.C. based CNN.com columnist Mark Shields shares a few self-effacing nuggets about Bush, who once said:

"These stories about my intelligence capacity do get under my skin a bit. For a while, I thought even my own staff believed them. There on my schedule first thing every morning it said, 'Intelligence Briefing.'"

Bush told of calling former Democratic National Committee Chairman and fellow Texan Bob Strauss for advice on "how I should deal with this perception (that I wasn't up to the job). Strauss said: 'Just remember, Mr. President, you can fool some of the people all of the time ... and those are the people you need to concentrate on.'"

Alluding to his verbal misstatements and mispronunciations, Bush said, "You know what Garrison Keillor said the other day? He said that 'George Bush's lips are where words go to die.'"

He owned up to some of his more publicized verbal gaffes at the prestigious White House Radio & TV Correspondents' Association dinner. Bush acknowledged saying things like: "I understand small business growth. I was one." Another: "I know the human being and the fish can coexist peacefully." But then he topped the laughs by explaining that "Anyone can give you a coherent sentence. This takes you to an entirely new dimension." With this add-on, Bush demonstrated a rarely mentioned aspect of self-deprecating humor. Calling attention to a mistake, a gaffe, or a weakness via humor is just the start. But if that's all you do and you do it often enough, it will just validate the perceived truth of what you're trying to overcome.

Self-deprecating humor is but a single weapon in your armament. Only use it when necessity beckons. It is a precious commodity. Rarely does it hit its intended mark. Too often it fails. So work it, practice it and hone it. It must, of course, pass the T&P lithmus test just as any other bit of workplace mirth. Don't overuse it. You know instinctively that nearly all humor is grounded in truth. Such it is with self-effacement. Just don't shine the light too long on your foibles or you're likely to hear something like, "Hey, now that you mention it, you really are a pompous jackass!"

Very few politicians understood the value of self-deprecating humor better than the late Morris K. Udall, D-Arizona, who ran for the 1976 presidential nomination, or U.S. Sen. Alan Simpson, R-Wyoming, who served as Senate Republican whip.

Mo Udall liked to tell about a time he was campaigning in the all-important New Hampshire primary when he went into a small-town barber shop and announced, "I'm Mo Udall, and I'm running for president," to which the barber quipped, "Yeah, we were just laughing about that."

Following the typical flowery introduction every senator is required to endure, Alan Simpson would quip, "Thank you, that's a lot better than the introduction I received the other night in Laramie (or Cheyenne, or Philadelphia), where the master of ceremonies said, 'Now for the latest goat from Washington ... Alan Simpson.'"

Nobody was better at using humor to deflect criticism of performance in office than Ronald Reagan. Criticized about his leisurely office hours, which rarely began before 10 a.m. and almost always ended before 5 p.m., Reagan confounded his critics with this line: "It's true hard work never killed anybody, but I figure, why take the chance?"

Self-deprecating humor should always be two-pronged. It should comedically acknowledge a criticism or situation, but also infer that there is no substance to it and that you're in the driver's seat. In a state of pique over an action taken by Gerald R. Ford, then Minority Leader of the House of Representatives Lyndon Johnson said Ford couldn't walk and chew gum at the same time. It was an angry and ill-considered attack on a popular and respected member of the opposition party. But the put-down assumed a life of its own and had to be addressed.

When Ford became president he began a speech at the Yale Law School by saying, "It's a great pleasure to be here at the Yale Law School's Sesquicentennial Convocation, and I defy anyone to say that and chew gum at the same time!" The audience loved it, it made all the television networks, and it showed a good-natured President Ford confidently turning around this mean-spirited jibe.

If you're a regular viewer of Saturday Night Live you'll remember Will Farrell's impersonation of then Secretary of State Janet Reno. Farrell, a 6'3", 230 lb. man, pretty accurately captured Reno's essence. Following a quickly growing group of politicians who have done the same, Reno appeared on the show, in a night club sketch dancing with Farrell's imitation.

Self-deprecation; it's the fastest way to an audience's heart. And you'll inch that much closer to earning authentic appreciation from your employees.

A few months before he passed away, Steve Allen gave a talk at the National Press Club in Washington. Steve was not in good health and his body was stooped over as he approached the lectern. He said the audience might have noticed his bent-over condition. He said it was an old football injury; yesterday he tripped over an old football. The audience's attention and concern about his appearance was put to rest.

Allen's anticipation of the public's opinion of him was fundamental to making the joke work. It all comes back to you knowing what your people are saying about you. Armed with this knowledge, you now have self-effacement ammunition to annihilate yourself in front of your employees. But remember to be moderate: Don't overdo it on yourself or you may lose their respect. If you harp on it enough, it'll become obvious that you are simply not worthy of leading them.

As rumpled and brilliant homicide detective, TV's Columbo would say, "One more thing." It's this: Self effacing humor must spring from an authentic conviction that you truly are deficient. In other words, if you're a pompous, arrogant JawClencher an attempt at public self-flagellation to ingratiate yourself with your troops will fall flatter than a one-eared tenor. Consider the somewhat obvious logic of the following:

> "A narcissist rarely engages in self-directed, self-deprecating humour. If he does, he expects to be contradicted, rebuked and rebuffed by his listeners ('Come on, you are actually quite handsome!'), or to be commended or admired for his courage or for his wit and intellectual acerbity ('I envy your ability to laugh at yourself!'). As everything else in a narcissist's life, his sense of humour is deployed in the interminable pursuit of Narcissistic Supply."
> SHMUEL (SAM) VAKNIN

Admittedly, the whole point of this book is for you to awaken your lighter side and use it to your advantage. But remember that we want to use that levity to affect positive and productive changes. If you are merely using humor to build yourself into an all powerful, self-serving office deity, you sadly have missed the proverbial boat.

CHAPTER 9

Practical Applications of Levity

"Public speaking is very easy."
Dan Quayle, to reporters in October 1988

The hallmark of any great speaker is the uncanny quality that enables said leader to inspire his or her followers to the promised land of zzzzzz. Sorry, I've fallen asleep just imagining how bored I get sitting through most presentations. Granted, that may have something to do with my ADHD, OCD, low blood sugar, and all the other ailments I'm convinced I suffer. But chances are excellent that you know what I'm talking about. Matter of fact, you might even be a perpetrator yourself of some real yawners.

In the company conference room, department meeting room, a sales meeting or at a trade show or industry conference, you simply cannot avoid public speaking. Here it is, your big chance to inspire (or perspire). Naturally you would opt to suffer cuticle torture than prepare for a presentation, much less deliver it. Your prep probably consists of spending hours putting together PowerPoint slides, leaving precious little time to map out your words. You worry about the technology-the computer, the projector, the microphone (if necessary), and your pacemaker. Data sheets, white boards, overheads, oh my.

Bottom line: You've got to be prepared. Know your material. Over prepare. Cover your butt. Confident that you've got it locked down, relax and forget about it. Only then will you be able to loosen up enough to keep your listeners from falling asleep on their forearms. Levity is the key.

But just to lay the groundwork of effective presentations, here are some fundamentals:

The shorter the better. Simply put, when people are slouching, yawning, or actually lobbing things at you, you've gone too long and it's time to finish. Rephrasing important concepts is fine as a wrap up recap, but avoid over-reiterating. Brief is best. Nobody likes a long speech, not to mention a presentation that's dryer than a Saharan cotton swab. Even if you possess a good sense of humor, less is more. If it worked once, then once is enough.

Don't be afraid to use notes. Using notes does not mean reading your remarks, word for word, off of index cards. Jot down a couple of bullet points and then succinctly make your case. And don't worry that notes look like a crutch; they are. Zig Ziglar, arguably one of the finest public speakers ever, uses overheads and notes. Flashcards, 3x5 cards, an outline on a single sheet of paper, speaker notes on your MS PowerPoint software, whatever. Use them; they'll help you stay on task.

Relax. It's just a presentation, not the end of the world. Have some fun. In *How To Get Rich,* Donald Trump says, "Before you speak, remind yourself that it doesn't matter all that much. Don't feel that the weight of the world is on you. Most of the people in the room don't care how well or poorly you do. It's just not that important." Remember that it's *your* presentation; nobody has any idea how it's supposed to go. If you neglect to say something or "flub," don't draw attention to it. The audience has no idea.

Keynotes, breakout sessions, training, and other corporate presentations can actually be engaging and entertaining. When you couple compelling material with a willingness to lighten up and take a casual approach, your presentation will be memorable. Once you've covered presentation basics, it's time to integrate some levity.

Let's look at some very helpful **dos and don'ts** when it comes to using humor in presentations as outlined by Herbert Prochnow in ***Requirements of a Good Toastmaster: The Complete Toastmaster***. Naturally, I've enhanced the list with my comments, like it or not.

Do *use humorous stories and jokes that relate directly to the topic of your speech.* Trying to boost sales? Tell a sales-related story or joke to begin with. Getting ready to talk to your accounting department? Topic-specific humor can be garnered from recent or past personal experiences, something you heard happened to someone else, a newspaper article, or even a joke book. The Internet is loaded with topic-specific humor. It's as simple as typing in the word plus "jokes" into your favorite search engine. Example: "secretary jokes" or "sales humor."

Don't *laugh at your own story or joke.* Really gifted speakers and comics can get away with it, on rare occasions, but they have an innate sense of timing and propriety. You probably don't. When in doubt, which is nearly always, keep a straight face when you score a laugh, and especially when you don't. If the only one laughing is you, you may as well skip to your close; you're done.

Do *laugh at your own story or joke.* On the other hand if the audience is roaring with laughter and you're standing there looking like you've just saved the world it smacks a bit too much of showmanship. Who are you after all, Jerry Seinfeld? No, you're Phil or Phyllis from Accounting and you just "made a funny." If it strikes you as amusing and others are laughing, then laugh if you feel like it. You're one of them, just a human. Not some well-traveled 100 bucks per night comic.

Don't *offend.* It goes without saying that your favorite one-legged pirate joke probably wouldn't be best if there's someone in the room with a prosthetic. Remember **Time and Place** along with **Necessity, Impact**, and **Consequence**. Something else to keep in mind is your own ability to improvise. The vast majority of people can't. It's just not part of their makeup. A quick wit, while mostly an innate gift, can be learned. Just not by you. And though it may seem contradictory to say so in this book, you just don't have the time to read, absorb, and internalize the kind of head-on commitment it takes to do it.

The point is that 85% (totally made-up statistic) of all offensive remarks are not planned; they just happen. Meaning: you've strayed from your prepared plan and tried to ad-lib some kind of comedy. And you failed because not only was it not even remotely amusing, but you unintentionally offended someone. So, if you can't think on your feet without unleashing a cuss word or social hairball, stop doing it.

Do make the story or joke clear and to the point. As with the whole presentation, brief is best. If you're able to directly relate your joke or story to the topic you discuss, chances are very good you'll already be clear and to the point. Here's an example from my own experience:

Me: *Becoming a levity leader isn't easy. It takes a lot of effort. You've got to be committed to the cause. A chicken and a pig are walking down the road together and the chicken turns to the pig and says, "You know, it occurs to me that between the two of us we have the resources to open up a really great breakfast diner."*

"How so?" the pig says.

"Well, I can provide all the scrambled eggs, poached eggs, eggs over easy, omelets, and eggs benedict," the chicken replies. "And you can contribute all the bacon, ham, pork, and sausage."

"Hmm," says the pig giving it some thought. "I have a problem with this plan."

"What's that?" the chicken asks.

"Well for you, it's a sacrifice," says the pig. "But for me, it's a total commitment."

While this isn't terribly funny on paper, I get laughs every time. Why? Because it's brief, easy to "get," and it applies to the idea of commitment.

Do *relate the story or joke to the audience.* Know your audience. I worked in radio for what felt like a hundred years and the entire industry is driven by demographics. When I was a morning show host at a country station, you can bet I skewed my humor to my audience. Blue-collar, workin' man, slightly low-brow, truck, beer and dawg jokes made up my material. I hated it. None of it was funny to me. But I knew my audience. Play to them, not to you. Are you speaking to a group of young, aggressive hot shots out to conquer the world or a bunch of soon-to-be retirees who've been there and done that? Are you addressing a bunch of accountants or account managers? More women than men? Vice versa? Use your head and whole lot of T&P judgment.

Do *speak audibly.* The command my old high school drama coach would repeat was "Project!" as in project your voice to reach the back row. What good is concocting a brilliant bit of wordplay if nobody can hear it? Attendees will wear themselves out quicker than usual if they have to strain to hear you. And if you're delivering compelling material punctuated by levity, they'll *want* to hear you. Speak up. Look at the people, not above their heads, and make sure that you can see all eyes, a good indication that they can see you.

Don't *repeat a story or joke that flops.* It didn't work the first time. What makes you think that it'll work the second time? Move on gracefully. In addition, don't blame the absence of laughter on your audience. I hate it when I hear someone say, "Come on, people, what's with you? This is funny stuff here." While that may or may not be true, if they don't laugh that's their prerogative. Move on.

Don't *repeat a story or joke that works. Once is enough.* There are few things more pathetic than someone returning to the same well again and again, hoping to draw another "easy" laugh. It simply doesn't work that way. A recurring theme is fine, if you're gifted enough to build on an initial laugh, but few people really know how to do that. Think David Letterman. He'll get a laugh early on and then weave it back in to ad-libbed bits throughout the show. But, by and large, you're not going to do that. A bit worked. Your audience rewarded you with their laughing approval. Great. Don't pat yourself on the back too long. Your story did what it was supposed to do at the proper time, so let it go.

Do *tell a story or joke about yourself.* Check the chapter on self-deprecating humor and apply with typical T&P care.

Additionally:

- *Physicality and gestures*: If you're anchored behind a podium you may as well distribute ear plugs, sleeping masks and airline pillows right off the bat, because people will be dripping sleep slobber within minutes. Get out front and talk to people. Move around some. Be careful to not wander aimlessly or make predictable patterns. You're not on guard duty, left, right, up the middle, left, right, up the middle, etc. Your movements should be motivated.

Without becoming Marcel Marceau, don't be afraid to add life to your story/joke by adding some hand and body gestures. If someone in your joke is carrying a tire under his arm, show it. Incorporate a few logical non-verbal communication gestures into your presentation. A simple head nod or raised brow from you can substitute beautifully for the few words they represent. Overdoing physical movement will not compensate for lame material, it will simply highlight it. The old adage "less is more" is forever applicable.

Before you begin take some deep breaths. Shake your arms and legs out. Loosen up. Stretch, if you're still able. This is a show. Sure, it's just business…show business. Don't forget this simple truth of speaking: IF THEY'RE LAUGHING, THEY'RE LISTENING.

Be visual and expressive, within reason. Find some range and variety in your voice. Speed up. Slow down. Look for natural breaks in your speaking. Occasionally stop talking and just let your last words linger a moment.

- *One-liners:* Ok, they're cheap and easy, so why not have a couple ready? Most bookstores will carry three or four collections of quick, painless quips broken down into subjects. One of my favorites is a book called "The Giant Book of Insults" by Louis A. Safian. Sometimes I'll just read a few pages to get me into a good mood if I'm down. Very funny stuff and only one of many other similar books out there.

- *Use vivid words:* In the Woody Allen film, *Annie Hall*, Diane Keaton's character, Annie, frantically calls Woody's character, Alvy, in the middle of the night. She is delirious because there is an enormous spider in the tub, and she can't sleep. Alvy's character charges back into the bathroom then returns seconds later looking for a shovel or a broom. He settles on a tennis racket. Annie asks, "What are you doing with that?" Alvy replies, "Honey, there's a spider in your bathroom the size of a Buick." A Buick. Not, "there's a spider the size of a *car*." Word choice. And how the word is said. Woody and others have the gift of simply making the language funny by how they pronounce and stress certain consonants or syllables, or the emphasis they use on certain words.

There are words that are funnier than others. Most words that include a hard consonant sound can be stressed to add a humorous sound. The hard "c" or "k" sound, like in Buick or corncob. The word "punt" is funny when spoken aloud. Another funny word is "thicket." It's just sounds funnier than "bushes." You get the idea. Remember your mental filing cabinet. Funny sounding words, alternative ways of saying everyday phrases, news items, sports teams, fad phrases and the latest jargon are all important files to tuck away in your cranial file folders to be accessed and unleashed at the right place and at the right time. The magic of levity is in the details and therein lies the difference between being merely adequate as a speaker and being truly unforgettable.

Levity In Meetings

Discretion is king in the conference room, but by and large this is one venue that could certainly use a good shot of mirth. The saddest result of most meetings is the unintentional, but very real, birth of new, baby JawClenchers and BrowKnitters.

A work meeting is like a breeding ground. The JCs and BKs multiply like viral bacteria, spreading their infectious gloom to any and all defenseless prey within their reach. Normal, healthy, levity-loving innocents enter the meeting den and sometimes within only minutes are cast under the spell of these boring bliss-breakers whose soulless and tiring tedium coupled with their riveted, serious glares fuel their victim's apathy. They are then led by the hand slowly down to workplace hell.

Like death to the tortured, often the only relief from the suffocating seriousness is the welcome embrace of sleep. A transgression of this magnitude, however, will be met with either the disapproving and disappointed headshake of a BrowKnitter, or the violent verbal flogging of the JawClencher, who would view your nap as a personal attack on his or her character. The options for survival are few. Embrace the evil and become one of them, or arise from the ashes like the Phoenix Cardinals and take a stand for levity.

The truth is, most people welcome humor and merriment in the board (bored) room. It is a skill that typically only the deft or the daft attempt to employ. Think about it. Last time you sat in a room with a dozen or so colleagues feverishly discussing marketing plans someone either belted a humor homer out of the park or melted down quicker than a Snickers in a trucker's back pocket. The good news is that either way, the meeting participants nearly always welcome all attempts at levity. There are relatively few gatherings that occur in meeting spaces where humor done right is unappreciated.

Remember the time-and-place rule. I can't possibly reiterate that enough. Remember the time-and-place rule. Ok, that's enough. Remember the time-and-place rule. That'll do, pig…

By now you understand that laughter loosens us up and allows ideas and conversation to flow more freely. If you're laughing you're awake and focused, blood is flowing, tears may flow, choking is commonplace. This is an effective and productive (literally) meeting.

If it's your meeting it is your responsibility to keep the tone light, but not frivolous. This will spring forth from your overall tone of levity. It's true, we're talking about critical business stuff here, but will it actually kill anyone? Which brings us to another very important principle in gauging the serious quotient in a meeting: Will the outcome of this meeting result in someone's death? Because that's really the only thing that should force BrowKnitting and/or JawClenching. Death. And many believe it's not so bad anyway. By contrast, if you're planning a sales pitch or debriefing staff on a conference you attended, or even—heaven forbid—reviewing numbers, there is plenty of room for levity.

As in all things business—**It ain't the end of the world!**

Ok, so it's a bit folksy and oversimplified. But you'll be at your best when you're relaxed, and your rough edges are smoothed over a little. Humor can do this. We've all heard the phrase "diffusing the situation with a bit of humor." And it's absolutely true. Just remember it only prescribes "a bit" of humor. Along with Time and Place remember moderation.

Less is more in meetings. Imagine Don Rickles jacked up on Red Bull conducting a budget review. It's not a stretch to imagine losing the real focus of the meeting while Mr. Rickles skats and beebops, slinging insults and one-liners up and down the conference table. Conversely, brows knitted so tight they force blood out of your eyes will also repel any real productivity.

Stay focused on the tasks at hand. Don't make humor an agenda item. Simply unfurrow your brow and allow levity to standby idling. In neutral. If the occasion arises and a sly comment is cracked, let it be. If it's funny, laugh. Allow others to loosen up. When they see your jaws unclench and that you view life as so much more than dollars and cents, useful interaction and participation will multiply. Your meeting will actually accomplish something. As you assign action items they will be met with more enthusiasm and less resistance. And another bonus: people will actually want to return to future meetings.

How often do you find yourself with a full house at your kickoff meeting and subsequent meetings are less than perfectly attended? By the time you're down to the nitty gritty of actual deliverables, three of you remain. You probably set a bad precedent right off the bat. You were either boring or insane. In other words a BrowKnitter or a JawClencher.

E-Levity

Let's make one thing perfectly clear. When it comes to voice mail greetings and e-mails nobody gives a darn about laughing. I mean, really, who has time for your lame attempts at humor? They just want to get to the "beep" so they can say what's on their mind. The key here is not trying to be funny. In other words, you don't want to tell a joke or do a funny voice. Just leave the greeting and be done with it.

On the other hand, if you can leave a memorable greeting or message by using levity, then you should. Levity in most communications is more amusing and memorable than just being funny. Here's a fairly typical example of someone trying to be funny.

You call your supplier with an urgent need to double this week's shipment. Here's the greeting on their end:

Supplier

Hey there, you've reached Haverly Brothers Paper Products, sorry we can't take your call at the moment, we're probably busy using our bathroom paper products right now, ha ha. By the way, you know I used to work as a lumberjack, but I just couldn't HACK it…so they gave me the AXE! Haahahahahhahahaaaa..ooooooh. But anyway, when the old beeperoo goes off, do your THANG. We'll return your call as soon as possible. So please leave a detailed message with your name and number and (sound of toilet flushing) Oh! Shouldn't be long now. Ha ha. (Beeeeeep)

You

(click)

Admittedly, it's a stretch, even for the truly obnoxious. But we've all heard greetings in this vein. Once again, the key is not to PUSH humor. Levity is the order of the day. Simply keep the tone light and informal. Here's a good example. The levity is so subtle it barely translates off the printed page:

You

"Hi you've reached John Thomas, or rather you've reached my voice mail; obviously if you'd actually reached *me*, we'd be talking right now. Please leave pertinent info and I'll return your call soon. Thanks."

Succinct. Nothing real serious *or* gut-busting there. Just a fairly straightforward, light-hearted little greeting. It's apparent that John is just shooting from the hip, he's got a pretty good sense of humor, and he's letting it show by not taking his greeting too seriously. It is a *greeting*, after all. How do you greet people face to face? Stone-faced, knit-browed, and tight-lipped?

Would you ever greet a client in person with same coldness you do on your machine? What about e-mails? Let's discuss some common problems with BrowKnitters and JawClenchers when it comes to memos and emails.

Far too often, this is the sort of email that arrives in our cherished Inbox.

> Subject: Messes in the break room!
>
> Dear employees:
>
> If the current trend of not cleaning up after one's self in the break room isn't soon curtailed and/or halted, the break room will be closed until further notice. Eating on campus is a privilege, not a right.
>
> Thank You,
>
> Chizbag Klempf

This whole memo smacks of a nostril-flaring, jaw-clenching, brow knitter. Ease up off the reins, big fella. A great way to lighten up with a message like this is to type it as you would actually say it. Re-read that memo aloud and you'll see what I mean. Nobody—not even true JawClenchers—actually talk that way. And "eating on *campus*?" Let's go ahead and remove the word 'campus' from our workplace lexicon, shall we?

Here's another.

> Subject: Team members on Frigsten project
>
> Dear Team Members:

Due to the unforeseen consumption of time required to complete our deliverables for the Frigsten Project, it has become exigent that all Frigsten team associates convene until said deliverables arrive at a satisfactory state, at which point, and no sooner, will the meeting adjourn regardless of the hour. Above-mentioned confab will begin at precisely at 5:00 p.m., EST. Leadership wishes to express regrets if associates are in any way inconvenienced by the potential duration of this work session.

Delwick Twitty, Project Manager

Just how difficult would it be to write something like this:

Subject: Frigsten project meeting

Hey Everyone:

Looks like we're going to have to stay late tonight to get this Frigsten deal complete. Sorry; it could be an all-nighter. I promise to ply everyone with junk food and drink. The harder we work, the sooner we can get home.

Thanks, see you at 5.

Del

This e-mail clearly comes from a manager that leads with levity. The tone of the message is still serious; there' s no joking when it comes to satisfying a customer. But wouldn't you be more likely to grind out a late-night with a positive attitude after getting this e-mail than the first one?

Remember, levity is just loosening things up a bit. You're simply trying to convey a lighter sense of perspective: relax the brow, unclench the jaw. It's just work. Nobody's dying today.

CHAPTER 10

The Wrap Up

Jim and Vern have worked together at Harman's Management Group for decades. Jim is the president; Vern the COO. Vern and his wife have longed shared a secret signal. (They're not alone; my wife and I have used this since we were dating.) It's three squeezes of the hand or three honks of a horn. Maybe three lights flashing from the porch. It's three of something, representing the words, I-love-you.

One day at the office after a heated disagreement over something or other, Vern and Jim each stormed to their adjoining offices to cool off. After a few minutes, and to his surprise, Vern heard three distinct knocks on his wall. He shook his head a little and grinned. Jim had used Vern's own "secret" message to apologize. Vern gladly rapped the code back to Jim.

Is there a small smile on your face? There sure were on Jim and Vern's faces. That's leading with levity.

Have you ever heard of Ty Brown? Probably not. He's not a movie star. He's not a politician. He's not a world-class athlete, or even village-class for that matter. But Ty Brown has something that at all of us who care about levity should pine for: a top-notch laugh.

His office is just twenty feet or so from mine and others' and frequently we get to hear his great laugh. It's truly inspiring. It has to be one of the best, jovial, authentic laughs on the planet today. It's never forced or fake. Ty's not an obnoxious, frequent laugher. It only happens when it's supposed to, and boy is it worth the wait. It puts a smile on our faces. It wakes us up. Doesn't matter what we're doing—dealing with a tough client, sorting travels expenses, or planning a funeral—one blast of that laugh brings needed perspective to the grind.

A person with a laugh like that could ask you to empty the contents of your purse or wallet into his hands "for the good of the company" and you'd do it. Look up "infectious" in the dictionary and you'll find a photo of Ty Brown laughing…and one of a leper colony.

Do you have a laugh like that?

Wherever you are right now, laugh out loud. Come on, just do it. See what happens. Tighten your gut and push out a guffaw. Where are you right at this very moment? On a bus? In your cubicle? An airplane? Would it be way inappropriate for you to laugh? If so, why?

You've got a built-in excuse for whatever response you get; you're reading a book. In fact it's a book about humor, so chances are great that it'll look and sound totally natural to those around you. And if you're all alone, well then you have no excuse.

So do it. Tilt your head back and let her rip. It may sound fake or put on. So what? Within seconds you'll feel a surge of authentic joy, possibly coupled with a degree of humiliation and shame. But you won't care, because that natural little rush is worth it.

And with any luck you'll "infect" someone else with your little laugh. It may spread a little among those around you, as infections do. When you hear a great laugh, it gets you going, doesn't it? On the other hand your little fit may be met with animosity.

Perhaps seated across from you there on the bus or in the waiting room is a fully engaged JawClencher named Frank. You know his name because he still hasn't taken off his work ID badge; that's only removed for the occasional shower. He's burning a hole through you with his deadly serious glare. And you can just read in his eyes, "Cut the laughs, pal, this is a doctor's office, not the USO!"

To which your eyes will seem to reply—with your own stare and a huge grin—"Lighten up, *Francis.*"

About the Author

Philosopher. Humanitarian. Pulitzer Prize winner. People Magazine' Sexiest Man Alive. Author and lecturer Scott Christopher would like to meet the guy who is all those things. A **Harvard MBA** and **PhD from Princeton** are two really important sounding degrees, but Scott got his bachelor's from BYU. And while he's no **Doctor of Workplace Humor** or **Certified Levity Facilitator**, or **even very smart at all**, Scott's held down a lot of jobs over the years where he researched his topic.

A self-described corporate outsider—having worked many years in the pretend world of television and film—Scott now sits at a cubicle and lunches 'round noon like the rest of the real world. Rejoining the workaday world Scott discovered a yawning divide between leaders who demand results and leaders who actually get them. Scott believes leading with levity can fill the chasm.

Scott's enthusiasm, energy and engaging wit make for unforgettable seminars and keynote speeches that touch hearts and split sides. A regular columnist for *Human Capital* magazine and contributing author of the best-selling *A Carrot A Day*, Scott also writes screenplays and acts in film and television. His next book is *Fatherless Fathers*. He travels from Salt Lake City where he works for the O.C. Tanner Company, evangelizing the power of a Carrot Culture. He lives with his wife (just one) Liz and five sons.

www.ingramcontent.com/pod-product-compliance
Lightning Source LLC
Chambersburg PA
CBHW022058170526
45157CB00004B/1399